GAY...
SUCH WERE SOME OF US

Stories of Transformation and Change

Edited by
David E. Longacre

HARVEST USA

A HARVEST USA BOOK

GAY...SUCH WERE SOME OF US
Stories of Transformation and Change

Copyright © 2009 by Harvest USA

ISBN-13: 978-1-935256-01-4

ISBN-10: 1-935256-01-7

Scripture quotations marked (ESV) are from The Holy Bible, English Standard
Version, Copyright © 2001 by Crossway Bibles, a division of Good News
Publishers. All rights reserved.

Scripture quotations marked (NASB) are from the NEW AMERICAN
STANDARD BIBLE®, Copyright 1960, 1962, 1968, 1971, 1973, 1975, 1977,
1995 by The Lockman Foundation. All rights reserved.

Scripture quotations marked (NKJV) are from The New King James Version,
Copyright © 1982, Thomas Nelson, Inc. All rights reserved.

Scripture quotations marked (NRSV) are from The New Revised Standard
Version of the Bible, Copyright © 1989 by the Division of Christian Education
of the National Council of the Churches of Christ in the United States of
America. All rights reserved.

Scripture quotations marked (NIV) are from the Holy Bible, The New
International Version®, Copyright © 1973, 1978, 1984 by the International
Bible Society. Used by permission of Zondervan. All rights reserved.

Cover photograph by Irene Maguire
Copyright © 2009 by Harvest USA

Published by L'Edge Press
A ministry of Upside Down Ministries, Inc.
PO Box 2567
Boone, NC 28607

Table of Contents

Preface

We live in a time when people believe that someone who experiences same-sex sexual attraction is "born that way" and cannot change. Many believe that to ask someone to change is wrong. This book presents the stories of individuals who testify to a different reality. This book is for anyone who is personally struggling with same-sex attraction and needs hope. It is also for friends and family who are disheartened by the decisions of loved ones to pursue a homosexual lifestyle and who need hope. It is also for anyone who wants to better understand that people can change and leave the homosexual lifestyle.

The individuals you are about to read about are real. In some cases, for personal reasons, they have asked that only their first names be used. Some have passed on to be with the Lord. Some are living for Christ in whatever ways they can and others serve on staff with HARVEST USA. The writers of these testimonies represent only a small percent of those who have come through the doors of HARVEST USA over the years, but are examples of the many life-changing experiences we have witnessed. They are a fraction of the people who have experienced change as a result of the work of Christ.

These accounts are snapshots of each individual's journey of faith. These are not complete biographies, but pictures of people on their journey. It is important to remember that, biblically speaking, individuals do not instantly arrive at the place to which God has called them. Before the Israelites took possession of the land promised to Abraham, they went through centuries of struggle. Between the time of the promise and its fulfillment there were years of slavery, disobedience and warfare. It was a time-consuming process.

The life of Jesus Christ provides another example of someone who went through a process to reach a goal. Jesus was tempted in the wilderness for more than a month and spent three years teaching and healing. He experienced a night of torment before a trial that spanned hours. His death was drawn-out. He lay in the tomb for three days before his resurrection. Two thousand years have passed since that time as he continues to spread grace to a sinful world. Why do we expect individuals to experience instantaneous arrival?

Spiritual growth is a journey that includes progression and regression. There is often a slipping back mixed in with forward movement. And so it is with individuals who struggle with same-sex attraction. They move forward in love for Christ, and then they slip back into old ways. Do not expect every person whose story is in this book to claim perfect obedience and complete change. Instead, realize they experience a struggle with sin while moving slowly in a "God-ward" obedience. They are no different than any one of us who struggles with sin.

Though not all the writers in this book embraced a homosexual lifestyle or even self-identified as "gay," homosexuality defined part of their existence. It was unwanted for some and embraced by others. No matter how it was acted on, homosexuality (or the desire and struggle) was the only way they knew to understand life – but then something happened.

God began to interrupt and, ultimately, to disrupt their hearts. Some couldn't escape the reality of the Christian training they had had or the love and concern of another Christian that God brought into their lives at a critical point. Some realized that what they had seemed dark compared to what friends, who seemed happier and more authentic, had. Others just realized that God had a different plan and was calling them out. Just as God told Abraham to leave behind his homeland – everything he knew – to go to the promised land, so God called these individuals out of an old way of living into a new one. In all cases it meant a change of life and direction that only comes through and by means of a community of other believers. It is through other believers that God's grace is most often and best revealed.

No one in this book was able to travel the road of change alone. They were all assisted by the love and mercy of other believers. Whether or not we struggle with same-sex attraction, this is a challenge to each of us to help those in need. May this book challenge you to step out in personal faith.

John Freeman, President
HARVEST USA

Editor's Note

This collection of true stories is meant to give hope and encouragement to anyone asking, "Can homosexuals really change?" This is the third volume in our *Proclaiming Truth and Mercy* series, a series that deals with questions surrounding Christianity, ministry, and homosexuality. It is not a polemic against those who argue that people who have same-sex sexual desires should simply embrace "who they really are" and pursue homosexuality. Instead, it is meant to answer the question of whether change is possible.

Stanton Jones and Mark Yarhouse point out in their insightful book *Homosexuality: The Use of Scientific Research in the Church's Moral Debate,*[1] that the change question is often framed in a way as to imply that if someone can't change, then no one can change. There is a universalizing of personal experience to prove pre-conceived assumptions about homosexuality. The argument is made that if someone cannot change, we must accept his or her behavior as morally acceptable. This argument is flawed since we would not say this about substance abusers or compulsive gamblers.

We also live in a world where simplistic views about change dominate Christianity. Many people think that homosexuality is simply a conscious choice and therefore homosexuals can choose to stop what they are doing. This view does not take into consideration the complexities of why people get involved in same-sex sexual behaviors. It does not understand the power of experiences to shape behavior, the dynamic of our sinful hearts or the power of temptation.

---

[1] *Homosexuality: The Use of Scientific Research in the Church's Moral Debate.* (Downers Grove, IL: Intervarsity Press, 2000), pp. 117-151.

People do not wake up one morning and say to themselves, "Hmmm, I think I might try being homosexual today…never thought of it before, but it sounds like it might be a good option." It is not that easy. People who are involved in homosexuality or who struggle with unwanted same-sex desires, do not make a single conscious choice to act as they do. It is a long complicated series of events and choices and consequences and more events and more choices. Coming to the conclusion you are homosexual is like watching a sunrise. Initially there is a faint glimmer and then it gets brighter and brighter until it is *obviously* daylight. When did you actually realize it was day? People with same-sex attraction have it dawn on them that they are so. To demand they choose differently is naïve.

Change is not easy and is difficult to quantify. Is a person changed because he no longer has anonymous homosexual encounters, but he still desires them? Is a person changed if she chooses a celibate lifestyle? Is a man changed if he gets married to a woman? What about someone successfully having a heterosexual encounter amid all the struggles? A definition of bisexuality confuses matters even more.

When we get down to the real issue in most people's minds, "Is homosexuality okay?" then the question of change becomes more heated. Change or lack of it is used as an argument to prove or disprove the Bible. The ability to change does not speak to the morality of a behavior.

The question that this book answers is whether some people can experience change in their homosexual desires and behaviors. It does not say it is easy. It does not say that everyone who wants to change will. However, it does show that some people have experienced change. This disproves the claims of many pro-gay advocates that homosexuals cannot change; some can and some have. If some can, then homosexuality is not innate and unchangeable.

There is substantial evidence that individuals can change their desires and behaviors regarding homosexuality. If you are someone who wants to change, then read these accounts and gain hope.

Several common themes run through these accounts. The one that I find to be most critical is the role of community and relationships. Not one person in this book found freedom over his or her sexual desires without the help of other people. The role of loving Christians in the lives of these individuals should be obvious.

As such, this book is all about relationships. I know personally the majority of the individuals who have shared these testimonies, and can affirm that God has radically changed their lives. Some of the individuals I have not met and some have died. As you read, you will find memorials written by John Freeman about several remarkable men.

May you be inspired and thank the Lord for his mercy – a mercy that is there for you and me as well.

David E. Longacre, Series Editor
Harvest USA

Such were some of you;
but you were **washed,**
but you were **sanctified,**
but you were **justified**
in the name of the
Lord Jesus Christ
and in the
Spirit
of
our
God.

1 Corinthians 6:11, NASB

1

Living a Double Life

Tim Geiger[2]

Living in the Dark

Do you not know that the unrighteous will not inherit the kingdom of God? Do not be deceived: neither the sexually immoral, nor idolaters, nor adulterers, nor men who practice homosexuality, nor thieves, nor the greedy, nor drunkards, nor revilers, nor swindlers will inherit the kingdom of God.

1 Corinthians 6:9-10, ESV

I wondered if the people in the congregation heard my voice tremble or noticed the longer-than-normal pause as I read 1 Corinthians 6:10. Could they sense my nervousness? My mouth was so dry and my heart beating so quickly that I found it difficult to continue reading the passage. I was never so glad – and so afraid – to sit down in my life.

Publicly reading the day's assigned Scripture was one of my responsibilities as a worship leader and lay preacher in the small Lutheran church in Philadelphia where I had grown up. I had come from a family that had been leaders in this church for nearly fifty years. Now, I was on the fast track toward seminary. And, I was simultaneously convinced, on the fast track toward hell. I was one of those men who practiced homosexuality – the ones who will not inherit the kingdom of God.

---

[2] Tim Geiger is the Director of the HARVEST USA Pittsburgh Regional office.

Not that I hadn't tried to break free from my homosexuality. Since the age of nine, when I remember first having homosexual desires, I knew what I was doing was morally wrong. My behavior displeased God. Time after time, I would act out. Time after time, I would repent and promise God that I'd never do it again. I'd ask him to forgive me and take away my desires. But I felt no more able to stop than I was able to understand why I was doing it.

I could never remember feeling comfortable as a male when I was young, even when I was three or four. I'm still not certain what went on during those early years, but I remember feeling much safer staying away from boys and doing typically "girly" things. Girls were my only real friends growing up. The boys at school never stopped picking on me, calling me "gay," "sissy," or "faggot." At the age of six, I had absolutely no clue what "gay" was – except that I knew it meant I was somehow different from all the other boys.

So, it became easier to put as much distance between me and them as I could. I became more and more isolated and self-focused as I grew up. Maturing physically but not relationally or emotionally, I yearned for an older brother or a father figure who would come alongside me and show me love and affirmation. I wanted some man to tell me that there was something good about me – something worth loving. But my separation from my peers prevented me from knowing the very affirmation and acceptance I sought. Often, I'd be so overcome with sadness and rage that I'd hide and sob my eyes out for an hour or more. Why wouldn't God give me what I so desperately desired?

The lack of relationship led to an increase in fantasy. Since I couldn't find what I craved in a real relationship, I imagined that I found it in my fantasy world. As I got older, got a job, and moved away from home, I finally had the freedom and money to explore sex with other men. My entry into homosexual sex was slow, because of fear of disease, shame, and guilt. Bit by bit, though, I threw myself into the gay sex scene. By age twenty-five, when I was on the fast track toward seminary, I was spending two or three nights a week in adult bookstores and gay bars looking for men whom I might use to fulfill my fantasies.

The good boy-who-would-be-pastor, so respectable and kind, so quiet and humble, was living a double life. While on the prowl for sex, I didn't care what anyone thought. I told myself it didn't matter. What mattered most was finding what I was looking for. But while under the gaze of my family and church, I cared greatly – no, make that *feared* greatly – what they might think. So, while around them, I maintained a façade of morality, responsibility, and being clean-cut.

What did I fear from the church? From my family? Mainly, I feared their rejection, their disapproval, their anger. I had so few relational anchors that I didn't dare risk these. It would be devastating if I failed in their eyes. So, I carefully insulated myself and on the surface lived a flawless life. I had to keep my secret safe! But oh, how painful it was to live a double life – always denying one side of my life to present the other convincingly.

Why was sex such a problem for me? At the time, I thought it was merely because I lacked self-control. Or because I didn't read the Bible enough. The real problem, though, was that I refused to submit to God's promise to meet all of my true needs and desires through Christ Jesus.

This is what I mean: I would turn to sex as a comfort, as a coping mechanism, when I experienced a sense of pain, suffering, or loss. Any disappointment or joy could set me off – a bad day at work, feeling unloved, feeling lonely (a big one for me), feeling hopeless (especially hopeless in believing God would never accept me), feeling tired (most of my sexual binges were at night). Even good things – like getting a raise, gaining a girlfriend, making a new male friend, or preaching a good sermon – could act as triggers because of the fear that the good feelings just wouldn't last.

I was allowing my feelings to rule my life and my relationship with God. I had lost virtually all touch with reality and was operating largely from the safe – if not confusing – confines of my own fantasy world, where my own happiness and freedom from pain were my highest and most noble goals.

In my late twenties, I was tired of the tension of the double life. I was just plain tired of life itself! After years of calling out to God, he still hadn't answered my pleas for help or so I felt. So, one Christmas night I swore that I was going to give up trying to live as the "good Christian." It wasn't getting me anywhere – all it did was make me feel guilty about feeling good. I told God that if what he said in Scripture was true, I'd still wind up in heaven. And if it wasn't, well, at least I'd be free from the tension!

So I stopped going to church, isolated myself bit by bit from my family, and just threw myself into the gay lifestyle. Then I began to realize that God was answering my prayer.

I began to feel even more tormented. Even in the escape of sex, I couldn't escape God's Spirit telling me, "You won't find what you're looking for by doing this. This is not who you are." I couldn't even enjoy the sex itself – even when I thought I was light years away from God, this refrain sounded in my heart and my mind with a deafening roar! I found no relief anywhere.

Over the course of the next several months, I lost my job, almost lost my apartment, and fell into deep debt and a deeper depression. Why wouldn't God leave me alone? Why did he care?

Living in the Light

And such were some of you. But you were washed, you were sanctified, you were justified in the name of the Lord Jesus Christ and by the Spirit of our God.

1 Corinthians 6:11, ESV

I had never understood this verse as pertaining to me before. Now, it became clear. There was indeed tension in my double life, but it was the opposite of what I thought. I had acted as though I was a gay man trying to live as a Christian, when in fact, it was the other way around – I was a *Christian* trying to live as a gay man. The difference may seem subtle, but it is about as subtle to me as a two-by-four.

For the first time in my life, I begin to understand who I was in Christ: washed, sanctified, and justified by Christ before the Father. Even though I had tried to lose myself in my sin, I couldn't because my nature – my true nature as a holy and dearly loved son of God – had to exert itself because of Christ's glory. I was looking for love, for affirmation, and for acceptance in the arms of men, but all the while, God offered me perfect acceptance, affirmation, and love in Christ. He loved me despite my wretchedness. He reconciled me to himself despite my rebellion. He made me a worshipper of him despite my idolatry. I did not stand condemned before him; rather, because of Jesus' work, I was a dearly loved child. In Christ, I have been freed to rest in God's love.

Even beginning to understand these things took time – in fact, years. The lifetime the Lord has given me will be spent learning how to live as a cleansed, sanctified, and justified son in Christ.

Bit by bit, the allure of the temptations to which I had succumbed for years began to diminish. The more I submitted myself to God and sought my peace in Christ no matter my circumstances, the less I felt that I needed to resort to sin to feel better. Bear in mind that God really didn't change my circumstances, which is what I had been demanding all along, but that he gave me his peace and contentment in the midst of my circumstances.

A little at a time, I began to worship God and not his creation (Romans 1). I learned that my pursuit of male sexual relationships was actually false worship, because through it I was trying to find meaning in my life. I thought that sex would give me that.

I pursued it in such a way that it was really a form of worship, because I believed it was so important I would risk everything for it. That kind of devotion can only be called worship. Worship is only to be directed at God.

As I began to understand worship, friendships with men became somewhat less threatening and more stable. Because I was not seeking meaning for my life in other men, I was able to have normal interactions with them. In God's providence, I was even able to marry a wonderful, godly woman and begin a family.

I would do a great disservice to the Lord and you if I didn't also tell you that this process of change was hard. It hurt. I continued to wrestle with temptation, because part of me still wanted to feel good, to feel happy, no matter the cost. There were times when it felt like death to deny my flesh the relief it craved. Repentance is hard – no doubt about it – because in repentance, we are called to turn away from all those rebellious, idol-laden coping mechanisms we've clung to for so long and to cling instead to Jesus Christ, not knowing how, or if, the pain or suffering will end. But it is precisely because of the fear of death that we remain in bondage to our sin (Hebrews 2:15).

We're not willing to let go of the "sure bet" that we think our sin is and hope instead for what is better by far in Jesus. When we're suffering, we believe the lie that it is better for us to have five minutes of relative pleasure than to call out to Jesus. After all, Jesus may not allow us to feel pleasure! Jesus may not take away whatever is causing our suffering, be it disappointment at work, perceived rejection in relationship, physical pain, or overdue bills. It may seem better to have five minutes of something that's a "sure bet" – something that will give us relief for a moment – than to risk further disappointment with the Lord.

I found that relief in sin isn't relief at all; it's merely an illusion. Sin never delivers what it promises. It only corrupts. It only destroys. Although in the moment we may feel some relief, as though we've bitten the bullet and gotten through, sin always leaves us feeling ultimately more devastated and more hopeless than before. It's a vicious cycle that we cannot break on our own. You and I lack what is necessary to overcome sin. Only the work of the Holy Spirit building our faith to trust in the love of God through Christ Jesus can break those cycles. That's why Jesus had to die! We weren't created to do it on our own.

The only way that any of us can live in repentance, in consistent victory over sin, is to call out to Jesus, who is able to sympathize with our weaknesses, and give us mercy and grace to help in our time of need (Hebrews 4:14-16).

God frequently works to change our desires and behaviors through our relationships with others in the church. A large part of that process of repentance is to bring others into your struggle. Don't keep it a secret! Pray for the Lord to open your eyes to see one or two godly men or women in your church or circle of friends with whom you might talk about your struggle and sin. The thought of telling someone may seem terrifying to you. There is always the risk of rejection. But is it a risk you will take as a step of faith? Do you trust Christ to work in and through others in order to give you mercy and help in your time of need?

Bringing someone into the picture means far more than simply confessing your sin; it means trusting that person with your heart – being accountable to someone with your disappointments, joys, hopes, and longings. If you struggle with sexual sin, this may be a huge effort for you. We tend to separate ourselves from others for protection and comfort. Nevertheless, the goal of an accountability relationship is to have the other person know the complete you well enough to challenge you when you engage in behavior that leads to sin. The goal in accountability should be to have someone who can proactively prevent sin by calling you to repentance before temptation takes root.

Bringing in other believers is important too, because they will be able to hold up Scripture to you as a kind of mirror, helping you to see yourself and your motives with increasing objectivity and obedience. In fact, Paul says that it is only in the context of the church that any of us matures spiritually and becomes more like Jesus (Ephesians 4:11-16).

The first men I ever told about my story were at HARVEST USA, the ministry where I now work. Even that was anxiety producing, because I had worked so hard to never let anyone know the complete me. God was faithful, however, and they didn't reject me. They didn't condemn me. The Lord used this to give me the confidence to confide in a few other men as time went along. The more people who knew my fuller story, the more people were praying for me and asking me how I was doing. Not everyone will receive your disclosure with joy and thanksgiving, but those who do are precious saints and gifts of mercy from the Lord.

It is my hope that my story has struck a chord with you. You are not alone in your struggle; there are people who can help you, perhaps even someone you know in your church.[3] Living a double life is a hellish way to live. Set your hope and trust on Jesus, asking for the courage to walk as he will direct you, out of loneliness and isolation and into his community. Only in Christ can any one of us leave behind a double life.

---

[3] If you feel as though there is no one with whom you can speak about your struggle with sexual sin, call HARVEST USA and speak with a staff person who will listen and offer some of the Lord's comfort. Check our website for contact information on the office closest to you – www.harvestusa.org.

2

Anything for Love

Carol[4]

Seeking Love

My parents used to fight all the time, or so it seemed. I think that they did the best they could raising us, but they had so much conflict with each other that they didn't have enough energy left for us. My dad moved out when I was ten; still, there were times when I felt he loved me. I never felt that my mother loved me. She never came to any of my varsity volleyball games. She laughed when I started my first period and didn't want me to have a bra when everyone else in my class had one. In short, I never felt encouraged and supported in areas that nurtured my femininity.

In high school, I realized that I was not and could not be in control of all the events in my life. I could study hard and make good grades, but I couldn't do anything about my family or make my parents love each other. I couldn't find the love that I thought I needed to find happiness.

I didn't feel God's love for me except through the Christians I knew. Although I believed that Jesus did the things he asserted, part of me didn't want to believe Christ's claims on my life because I felt I would be leaning on a crutch. In spite of this, I came to accept Jesus as my Savior. My life quickly changed in two ways: First, I stopped swearing. Second, I stopped fighting with my brother.

---

[4] Carol came to HARVEST USA during the early years of this ministry and has asked us to use only her first name. Please note that those who have asked to use only their first names are not ashamed of what God has done for them, but make the request to protect family or children from potential ridicule.

I also moved in with a Christian family. I wished I could stay there for the rest of my life. The parents loved each other, the children got along, and for the first time I felt somebody actually cared about me. This family helped me see what God desires for families. It was a healing time, but it could not last forever.

Seeking Friends

Subsequent to this time of healing, life continued to change. After graduation I took a job that eventually led to a pivotal event. My company transferred me to a new city where I didn't know anyone. I felt very alone. I began going to church but never seemed to find a close friend. My heart yearned to share my loneliness, fears, and frustration with someone.

I did, however, get close to an older woman, who seemed very mature and self-confident (characteristics I lacked). I had heard rumors that she was gay but didn't want to believe it. Then, several months later, she told me so herself. I began to be afraid that I would lose her friendship if I didn't become sexually involved with her. Within a few weeks, we were living together as a couple.

I tried to convince myself that this was okay. After all, we did love each other. I tried to find some kind of approval from God. But because I wanted so badly to be loved, I felt like I was living two lives. I was one person around my family and people from church and another person around my lover and gay friends. All along, the real me was confused and lonely, looking for love anywhere I could find it.

The relationship lasted until she was transferred. Before long, I was involved with another woman. This time I couldn't fool myself into thinking I loved her. Deep down, I knew I was just using her to meet my needs for acceptance, affirmation and affection – things I thought were "love."

When I got up the courage to tell another woman friend of mine – who was not gay – what was going on, I braced myself for her reaction. I was terrified. Much to my surprise, she shared that she had already guessed what I was dealing with. She also said she knew where I could get some help. I began talking with a counselor who specialized in my problem. This step marked the beginning of the end of my involvement in the gay lifestyle.

I began to see myself as a woman who felt deeply inadequate and who had become an expert at covering up with an air of self-confidence. I had been playing a part (whatever the other person needed) for so long that it took a while to see the real person inside me. The real me was lonely, isolated, and constantly craved love. I, like many in the gay lifestyle, had become driven. I was like another friend who had told me that because she was gay she had to be "better to be equal."

Finding Love

My journey out of homosexuality was not easy, but I knew God wanted me to pursue it. I attended groups designed to help people coming out of the gay lifestyle. There, I found people who were going through the same process I was. This was a great support to me.

All through this process, God was faithful to me. He provided good Christian friends with whom I could share my struggles and heart in a wholesome way. I realized that in the past I had tended to become dependent on friends and to look for the approval of others to gain self-worth.

One of the things the Lord taught me was that he is to be the source of my sense of worth. I can know that I am a valuable person because he created me and I am a child of the King. I am not the person I used to be and don't need to be "fixed up" with someone to experience peace. He really does know my needs, and how best to meet them. There are always problems when I attempt my own strategies. I think I know better, but my methods never work. Learning to trust God is a faith issue. It can be very difficult, but I'm growing in this and he is being faithful.

Finding a Friend

A few years later, I was relocated through another transfer. The first night I visited what was to become my new church, I met the man God was to eventually provide as my husband. At first I thought we were just going to be good friends. We went places, saw movies, and talked and prayed together. The thing that amazed me was that this was a fulfilling relationship. I could begin to see that this was the way God meant intimate relationships to develop and evolve.

I realized that if I really wanted our friendship to be more permanent, I would have to tell him about my past and how the Lord was dealing with me. I don't remember much about the details of that conversation except that I found myself telling him that if he wanted out of this relationship, now was the time.

I do remember his response, however. He said, "I'd be a fool to leave you now. If you want to cry, you can cry. If you need to talk about it, you can talk about it, or it never needs to come up again." Then he gave me a big hug. We became engaged and were married several months later.

God has been so faithful to me. I see over and over again that God brought this man into my life; a man who listens and doesn't judge but rather looks for ways to encourage me and build me up.

Although there are people in the church who are afraid of

people who have been involved in the gay lifestyle, others are willing to love us and give of themselves. We need people to be role models for us. We need people who will talk with us when we need to talk and love us for who we are, with all our needs and inadequacies.

My growth continues. I have not "arrived" by any means. At times I feel that my growth is too slow. Yet my faith is in God and my hope in Christ, of whom the Bible says, "...he who began a good work in you will carry it on to completion until the day of Christ Jesus" (Philippians 1:6, NIV).

3

Looking for Love in All the Wrong Places

Ed LeClair[5]

Looking for Love

In the past few years, my life has included a variety of changes that I once could never imagine taking place.

My problem with homosexuality began approximately forty years ago, when I was a teenager. Life was very difficult. My formative years were those of confusion, loneliness, and parental psychological abuse. I never seemed to be able to measure up to my father's expectations and the estrangement between us lasted all his earthly life. Anger, pain, and bitterness grew inside me, and I carried them silently wherever I went. My view of masculinity became distorted. I longed for friendship with other men, but deep down always felt unable to relate to them in a normal way.

What followed were years of lying, covering up, and doing whatever I had to do to persist in this sin. It became addictive and I couldn't seem to live without it.

I seemed to be always "looking for love in all the wrong places" to fill the void. My life became a nightmare. I constantly and frantically searched for something that I could never find.

I thought it was all hopeless and got to the point where I dreaded waking up, knowing that all I was going to face was emptiness in my soul. I didn't fully realize that my separation

---

[5] Ed LeClair serves on staff with HARVEST USA as Development Director. He took this position after years in the secular business world. He has also served as a volunteer with HARVEST USA and on the Board of Directors.

from God was the source of my misery, but I was slowly becoming aware of my spiritual need.

As I began to think about my relationship with God, he did a wonderful thing. As I thumbed through the pages of a local Philadelphia magazine, I came across an advertisement for Harvest USA. It said that people who wanted out of the lifestyle should call a certain phone number. It said nothing condemning homosexuality, but simply appealed to those in need. A few weeks later I called the number.[6]

Found by the God of Love

When I called, I was immediately struck by the friendliness of a caring and seemingly understanding voice on the other end of the line. I knew that I had to visit the office and find out more. Through attendance at weekly meetings I began to draw on a strength that I never knew was available. The source of the strength is explained in Philippians 4:13: "I can do all things through him (Christ) who strengthens me" (ESV). This verse continues to ring true for me. My view of myself and my masculinity has changed.

Through subsequent involvement with Harvest USA, my relationship with the Lord has flourished. I became involved with other Christian groups and got Christian counseling. At long last my struggle was over, and the simplicity of it all astounded me.

But my life today is not easy by a long shot. Nor do I expect it to be. There are still problems with my family, and I continue to live with enormous pressures at home and on the job, but I see a

---

[6] When Ed first sought help with his struggle, he made the call from a public phone booth. The booth was the old-style glass box with the folding doors. Right after the call was answered and someone began to talk with him, he was no longer alone in the phone booth. He was mugged and had his wallet taken. He lost the information he had about Harvest USA and did not call again for a week or so. This incident reveals there is often a spiritual battle occurring when someone seeks help. – Editor

discernable difference! I no longer bear these things alone; God is with me. I also realize that God will not allow me to be tempted beyond what I am able to bear. Living, no matter how difficult, makes so much more sense now that I have a clear direction and wonderful goals to achieve.

Jesus Christ is my focus and my salvation. I once thought of myself as the lowest form of human life; now I realize I am quite valuable. I can make choices based on having as much to offer as any other man. I am accepted and loved in the truest sense. I am no longer separated from God, and he does not condemn me. This truth is simple but genuinely liberating to a person who has had to struggle with homosexuality his whole life.

I thank God every day for the wonderful work of HARVEST USA and for making me a part of it. The fellowship, true caring, and friendship (along with the steady leading of God) have opened my eyes so that nothing seems hopeless anymore. I am one person who has conquered this battle and lives in constant wonder at the healing power of Jesus Christ. I highly recommend him for everyone!

4

Silent Sisterhood

Irene Maguire[7]

Sisterhood?

What I want to share is not so much the story of how and why I wanted out of the homosexual lifestyle, but rather what has happened to me since. I will not pretend to have answers to all the questions. This is a story of "a work in progress" and how God ceaselessly and actively works in my life.

I came to HARVEST USA because I was convicted that there was something very wrong in what I wanted from people and women in particular. I remember the night I finally began to see the subtle differences in what was good and bad in my friendships. It was at a New Year's Eve party to which a certain few were invited. As I sat there I was aware of (as if for the first time) the lingering, meaningful gazes, the exclusive conversations, the private jokes, the hand resting too long on the shoulder, and the feeling of being sucked into something that was no longer alluring. Everything worked in this group by hints and insinuation; nothing was ever said openly, so nothing could be defined. I remember it being a long, long night.

The next morning I spoke to someone who shared with me her New Year's Eve evening. She talked about how she and her friends had come together and prepared a meal. Then during

---

[7] Irene Maguire, who is Irish by birth, has been the Office Administrator at the Philadelphia office of HARVEST USA since 1999. Irene also speaks at colleges and in other settings, sharing her faith and providing insight into what it means to be a daughter of Christ.

that meal they renewed their friendships and prayed for the coming year and what it would bring. I walked away from her into another room – and cried. The openness and honesty of the events of her evening contrasted sharply with the complete lack of anything meaningful in mine and cut me to the bone. The "Silent Sisterhood" to which I belonged required secrecy, and for maintaining the secret my reward was an aching hollowness that gnawed deeper and deeper into my soul. I was a living, breathing lie. I had spent a lifetime building a pleasant, inoffensive façade keeping all but a tiny few out. Now this façade was so thick that it seemed impossible to break through. This is a testimony, however, that God can pulverize even the thickest walls around our hearts.

If God says to me, "No, this is not the lifestyle to which I call you," then to what does he call me? There is more to living than just not being gay anymore. For me, HARVEST USA is not just about bringing men and women out of the homosexual and lesbian lifestyle. It is a mistake to think that when someone stops acting out the gay lifestyle that it ends there. In many cases all you've got is a celibate homosexual or lesbian who lives in an androgynous twilight world of simply knowing what shouldn't be done. It's a cold, comfortless place to be.

Those who stop there find little to rejoice about; their hearts are rarely open or warm, and their anger, something to avoid. So, as I came to know what I shouldn't do, my heart cried out to God to know what he was calling me to be! There had to be more. My heart yearned too much for these deep changes to stop there. What was it? What was it I was tasting and glimpsing, that drew me closer and closer to the edge? God drew me to the cliff edge of making choices, and to the realization that I had choices. It was in this place I first began to understand what it was to be a child of God – the child of a loving father.

Being a Daughter Instead

Though it sounds simple, to move from seeing myself as a child of God to being his daughter was a momentous step. I could easily have held on to the idea of being a child; seeing myself simply as a child. But if that was the only image I held onto, then for the rest of my life I would have never effectively grown up. However, God calls me to be his daughter – his beloved daughter – and to grow into womanhood, capable of seeing and experiencing him, people and life in a totally unique way through my femininity. He teaches me in his Word and leads me to women in church, in groups and in friendships who, as in the words of Proverbs 31, are clothed in strength and dignity, who do not fear the future because of him and who speak with wisdom and faithful instruction. These women move freely, enjoy the respect and confidence of others, and shatter my old notions of strength, independence and freedom. These women are interdependent. They do not see themselves as separate; they are connected closely to others and enjoy it. This connection is neither smothering nor exclusive as in lesbianism, but springs from being present to one another even in the hard, raw times that God uses to shape his daughters.

I am at that point of my journey where I have begun to explore this part of me, and it is not without fear. I am often frightened by the newness of everything. In a world in which I have heard femininity described as a ragbag of discarded female values to be passed over in search of something better, allowing my life to be shaped by God through his gift of femininity is frightening. To expose myself to the refining fire of my Father, to feel the sharpness of his knife as he cuts deep into the shadowy corners of my soul exposes that fear for his attention so that he may deal with it. And I also know this: that God sets me on a high cliff and there I feel his breath – it can burn like fire, searing through me and separating sinew from bone, but as I come apart he reshapes me for his purpose. The protection of his love holds my feet firm. Only God protects and gives safety as I look on things long buried and discarded that I am now willing to pick up and own as part of me.

From the safety of his protection I face the temptations to go back and strive at being strong and independent, and consequently to be untouchable in the core of myself. These temptations are still there, but in God's love I no longer welcome them as old friends but see them as the soul destroyers they are.

My femininity, my sexuality, my place as a daughter, these are all gems for the taking from my Father's hands. How I will wear such precious gifts is something that only time can reveal. But as I look on these well-cut stones, their facets catch and reflect the light of my Father's love. The luster of his promises never fades. They are promises more enduring than the hardest diamond. They are promises worth dying for – and Christ died so that I might receive these gifts. To receive is something that was impossible for me not so long ago. There is beauty in this that I know I am just beginning to understand. God has lifted the curtain and I have glimpsed something wonderful that promises more. I want to know, see and be more of what he is calling me to be. As he reveals more, I know this process will not end in this lifetime, but it is a journey I want to make. I want to make it hoping and trusting always in him, my Father and his love for me.

5

Healed in the Heart

Steve DeVries[8]

I was brought up in a typical middle-class home on Long Island, NY. It was at about age thirteen that I had my first homosexual experience. Although at that time it seemed an innocent and isolated occurrence, little did I know the devastating effect if would have on my life.

Those early experiences led to fifteen years of guilt and confusion. A move to the West Coast to attend college brought new "freedoms" that were damaging. The move enabled me to seek out gay bars and begin involvement in the gay lifestyle. This was something the small farm community from which I had come had not afforded.

Never willing to face the real loneliness of my life for very long, I found temporary peace in new surroundings. Los Angeles, San Francisco, Las Vegas, south Florida and a year in Europe only enabled me to keep running away. I thought that I could find happiness in a constant stream of new people, new places and new things. Although I was getting more involved in the lifestyle, I was still conscious of enough confusion to seek out psychiatrists. I found out that the psychiatrists often needed psychiatrists.

During this time, I also tried to push myself into heterosexual relationships, at times getting serious enough to come through with promises and diamond rings. I never could go through with it. Those years were characterized by guilt and misery.

---

[8] Steve DeVries came to HARVEST USA during its early years, and his life has left a lasting impact on our ministry.

By the age of twenty-eight, I just gave in. I rationalized and made the necessary excuses. I said, "Well, this is the way God made me and wants me. I'm a homosexual, and I'll have to live with that for the rest of my life." So I dove into that for the next fifteen years. Along the way I learned that alcohol dulled the pain (and hidden guilt). I escaped having to "feel" and lived day-to-day in relationships (of differing durations) that often meant nothing.

Still looking for that ultimate "pain killer" at age forty, I got into crack, one of the most deadly drugs on the market. I don't know how, but I did find success in business and money. I had all the material trappings of a successful yuppie. As a businessman, I was making a ton of money. Then the bottom began to fall out. I was arrested for coke possession, spent one night in jail but was released in the morning. Within a month I was arrested for possession of crack again. This time it hit the headlines of the newspaper in the small south Florida town in which I lived and worked. I was fired from my job and began a prison term.

I remember sitting in prison, contemplating and even planning my suicide. I began to pray for the first time in a long time. I prayed that God would do something. I had lost everything. I got involved in AA and various drug programs and became substance free. But I knew that still was not enough.

As part of my parole, I landed a job in the Philadelphia area. I began to frequent gay bars again, but something wasn't the same. I didn't drink but would just sit there and look at all those lonely people. Only, somehow, I now couldn't relate. Now I felt completely lost. "This is the only thing I've known. What am I going to do now?" was all I could think. It was about this time that I read an ad in the newspaper for HARVEST USA, which said there was help and hope for people like me!

Thank the Lord I found that ad. I called up the number and went in and talked with John Freeman. He listened for a long time and then told me about Christ and how Jesus really cared about me and my problems. During that first appointment, I accepted Christ into my life.

It's hard for me to understand and explain, but after that my life changed dramatically. I began reading the Bible, praying, and developing a personal relationship with Jesus Christ. I had always known deep down that there must be some purpose to my life. Now I knew! Perhaps the biggest change has been that the loneliness and insecurity that plagued my life are gone. I'm a new man in Christ, and the Lord is my personal friend. It's really unbelievable. No crack or cocaine can come near it.

In January 1989, about six months after giving my life to Christ, I faced a new problem. That month I went to the dermatologist to check out a patch of skin on my face. It turned out to be Kaposi's sarcoma. Tests revealed I had AIDS. I have since begun the AZT treatment and the whole medication thing.

The Lord may heal me or he may not. That's not in my control. The important thing is that the Lord is enabling me to deal with this – he and my new Christian friends. Even my own family has been extremely supportive. On a recent trip home, my parents, though not Christians themselves, perhaps summed it up best when they told me, "Steve, it really doesn't matter if the Lord heals you or not. The crucial thing is that you're healed in your heart!"

In Memoriam

John Freeman

Steve DeVries, a brother in the Lord who left an impact on all the lives he touched, died on September 2, 1992, in Glens Falls, NY, with his family at his bedside. He was mourned by everyone at HARVEST USA.

I first met Steve in October of 1987 when he responded to an ad that HARVEST USA had placed in a newspaper, seeking to reach those who wanted out of the gay lifestyle. I remember especially how humble Steve was during his initial interview. He was particularly aware of how he had been trying to gain some sense of wholeness and meaning through his homosexual involvements, only it was not working anymore.

During that meeting I sensed that the Lord had his hand on Steve in many ways. Steve began asking all the "right" questions about his need for something deeper and more foundational. As I shared the Gospel with Steve and explained what the life and death of Jesus Christ had to do with his problems, I could sense a light going on. Steve ended up asking the Lord to come into his life that day!

The next two years for Steve were filled with growth and fellowship. He had attached himself to a local church and was involved in its life. Yes, he still struggled, but intent on walking a life of obedience, he had given the Lord the position of "boss" in his life. For all intent and purposes he had chosen to get his needs met through the Lord and his relationships with other believers, not through the gay lifestyle.

Almost two years after our first meeting, Steve dropped into the office for a surprise visit. Within a few minutes of sitting down with another staff member and me, Steve burst into tears; this was not like Steve. A successful businessman, at the age of forty-two he had a confidence and sense of security combined with an inner sense of control that didn't leave much room for displays of emotions. A warm and sensitive man, yet outwardly always quite controlled, this outburst signaled that something was drastically wrong.

Steve told us that, having not felt well for several weeks, he had gone to a clinic to see if he might be carrying the HIV virus. The test was positive. The three of us wept, and even then Steve managed to vocalize his awareness that God was with him in this and would not abandon him. God had brought him this far and would not let him go.

As Steve displayed more symptoms of HIV disease, he turned to a local ministry that assisted AIDS patients and began to face the realities of this deadly disease. In a mature and methodical way, he began to "tie up the loose ends" of his life in the Philadelphia area and prepared to move back to his parents' home in upstate New York. With a sense of sadness we said goodbye knowing that Steve had come to occupy a special place in our hearts.

Back in his hometown and still in relatively good health, he made the necessary medical contacts that would increasingly become a part of his life. He told me about an initial visit with a physician. Sensing the need to talk about Christ with this doctor, Steve explained to him just how he had come to know the Lord and how Christ had given him the power to break from his homosexual lifestyle. The doctor was taken aback by Steve's testimony and expressed his sorrow that now that Steve had AIDS, he was feeling guilty and seeking change. The doctor implied that Steve's faith was a reaction to getting AIDS and had little to do with him leaving the gay lifestyle. Steve corrected the doctor, explaining that his encounter with the Lord and his changed life had happened several months prior to the HIV diagnosis.

Steve soon became involved in a local AIDS support group with the idea of not just getting support for himself, but of focusing on how the Lord might use him to touch others with the same grace he now knew. Within a few minutes of the first meeting, Steve quickly saw that most of the people in the group were gay men with HIV. During the sharing time, as the men went around and shared how they were dealing with the disease, Steve spoke of how he was coping, where he had come from, and what God was doing in his own life.

Predictably, the others immediately reacted with hostility, anger, and contempt. Several men told Steve not to come back to the group and that they did not need his kind of "preaching." But Steve did go back, withstanding the mistrust and unpopularity his initial introduction to the group caused. He just kept going back.

As the men in the group observed his tenacity in handling his disease in a way that maintained his dignity and yet was rooted in his relationship with Christ, they slowly warmed to him. On one occasion Steve phoned me from his home on a Sunday afternoon to ask me to pray. He was in the middle of a cookout and twenty men from his support group were there. Although still resistant as a group to their need for redemption and grace, one by one many of the men had sought Steve out privately to spend time with him. During these times he tried not only to be a friend, but to minister the Gospel in word and deed.

Being a Christian did not mean that Steve escaped the pain and suffering associated with HIV disease and AIDS. He simply had a supernatural way to deal with it. One entry in his diary contained the following solace, which came to comfort his soul on many occasions: "When I feel pain, I think about the Lord and the pain goes away. When I'm frightened, I think about the Lord and I'm not scared anymore. When I am lonely, I think about the Lord and the loneliness goes away."

During the last two years of his life, our staff had continued contact with Steve. He wrote and called us regularly. He gave his testimony in 1990 to a room full of 250 people. He joked about my having told him to keep his talk to ten minutes and his response that since he had driven seven hours to get there, surely I would not mind if he took longer! That was Steve! He was always hard to contain when it came to his talking about the Lord.

I spent time with Steve at a lodge in Adirondack, New York, during the two summers before his death. With particular fondness I recall sitting out in the darkness around the campfire. The cool night air and total darkness stood in stark contrast to the millions of bright stars. Steve spoke of his growing intimacy with the Lord and how the Lord had taken care of his every need. Then I realized I was a bit envious of his constant recognition of God's faithfulness and grace. His dying process and coming to terms with the end of his life only seemed to expand his reflection on and appreciation of the sovereignty and grace of God. My own day-to-day awareness of these truths seemed dull in comparison.

A few days before his death, Steve took a turn for the worse and refused all medical interventions to prolong his life. Alert and of quick and sharp mind almost to the end, Steve went to be with the Lord peacefully.

It is my hope that you will remember Steve and think about his trust in the love and compassion of Christ. I hope you will be challenged to tell others about your own walk with the Lord and speak about his mighty deeds everywhere you go. Most of all, I hope you see the "what if" possibilities in the unbelievers around you. Envision what that person could be if he or she knew the love and grace of the Savior. Christ is able to change anyone he touches with his grace. Realize that you have the privilege of sharing that message out of your own sense of brokenness and gratitude to Christ.

6

An Extravagant Love

Kristin Patterson[9]

Before I was born, my father left my mother, my two brothers, and me. My mother soon spiraled into alcoholism, which resulted in two of us being placed in foster care when I was four years old. It didn't take long for me to realize that "foster care" was just another word for "unwanted." I concluded that there must be something deeply wrong with me to cause my mother to abandon me, and soon viewed myself as a girl who was worthless, unloved, and unlovable.

The flip side of taking on that identity was the belief that everyone else must be valuable, loved, and lovable. That fueled an intense jealousy of other girls who had parents who loved them, friends who enjoyed their company, and who had an intrinsic value. In the midst of this, I clung to the hope that my mother was coming back for me and fantasized about her rescuing me from foster care. I believe my struggle with same-sex attraction began with this consuming jealousy of other girls and fantasy of woman as savior, rescuer, and hero. If my mother was not going to rescue me, then maybe another woman could.

These beliefs became twisted into worship of other girls and older women who I thought possessed everything I did not. I easily slid into a posture of adoring and emulating these people so I could somehow possess what they did. Mine was a classic case of "cannibal compulsion." I believed that nearly every other girl was better than me in some way. I wanted to be near them and consume their best traits. The closest I could get to being them was to engage in a physical relationship with them.

---

[9] Kristin Patterson is a pseudonym.

To make matters worse, an older female cousin had already introduced me to pornography and initiated sexual play. By the time I was ten a foster father had molested me. When I was thirteen our youth pastor cornered me in church and kissed me. These incidents contributed to a severe distrust and fear of men, and solidified my feelings of attraction to women.

By this time I understood that I really did prefer girls over boys. Although I didn't stop acting out with boys, I was developing a habit of allowing friendships to become sexualized, either in my mind or in reality. I hated my behavior but craved the attention and physical connection. Compounded by the shame of being attracted to other girls, my sense of alienation and isolation grew much worse when I was a teenager.

I became more and more depressed, began drinking and cutting myself, entertaining suicidal thoughts, hiding crushes on my girlfriends, and acting out sexually with my "boyfriends." I never felt I belonged anywhere, and by now I was so different even on the inside that I despaired of ever finding a place to fit in. Not having much connection with my natural family and feeling on the outside of my foster families, I looked for community and family among my friends. I thought I could get every need met in them.

I knew that what I was doing wasn't right. I had asked the Lord into my heart when I was six and attended church in the different homes I lived in, gone to Christian camp, and even attended a Christian school. I just didn't know how to stop my behavior. By the time I was a junior in high school I was torn between the two sides of me. One part desperately wanted to be a "good girl" and lead a "good" Christian life, but another part really needed (and liked) the attention I was getting from my lesbian friends. I found pleasure in the "forbidden" aspect of these relationships. My secret life set me apart, made me different, and most of all, gave me comfort that nothing else did. My relationships with other girls seemed to be my only source of acceptance, affirmation, and affection.

I also believed there was a battle being waged over me. I was a bright kid and spiritually observant, so I knew that spiritual warfare was real. I wanted so much to belong to God and be claimed by him; but I believed Satan had claimed me first and would never let me go. Convinced I was more his than God's, I became hopeless and despaired of ever being released from the oppression.

When I was seventeen, I spent two weeks in a psych ward for major depression. The first night was the hardest. I felt completely abandoned and alone. I believed I was a huge failure. I prayed that night and told the Lord that if he wanted this mess of a life he could have it. I gave my life back to the Lord, had great fellowship and discipleship my senior year of high school and even went to a Christian college

The first half of my freshman year went fairly well. I tried to spend time reading the Bible, making Christian friends, finding a church, and getting involved in ministry. But I met a sophomore to whom I was immediately attracted and I could not let go of the desires. I did not know what to do with my continued attraction to women. What made it more difficult was the pro-gay theology that the school promoted. I wanted more than anything to believe that I could live a bisexual lifestyle and still love and please God.

I had never talked about my struggles with anyone until I went to college. When the inner battle erupted that year, I decided to meet with a student leader and confess what I was struggling with. I poured out my heart and when I was done she said, "Don't worry, you'll grow out of it."

That was it.

I couldn't believe it.

In my heart I knew she was wrong. I also knew I was wrong for acting on my desires, and it made me angry that she would not tell me the truth. I wanted someone to give me a good enough reason to change. Not even the campus counselor would tell me that homosexuality was biblically wrong.

I was part of the Evangelicals for Social Action chapter at the college and at one of our meetings a guest speaker presented a seminar on homosexuality. Needless to say, he supported the theory that homosexuality was a genetic trait and therefore a natural form of sexual expression that Christians should be allowed and encouraged to pursue. That was exactly what I wanted to hear. If these older, wiser Christians were teaching this, how could it be wrong? I went home for Christmas and decided that I was done fighting. I was just going to choose women for good. I had sought counsel, I had sought the Lord, and the responses I had gotten were so lacking that I finally gave up and gave in.

I had some crushes, a few short relationships, and some one-night stands. After a year I was feeling even emptier, more desperate, and unsure that this choice was going to help me find myself. I discovered an unsettling truth: the more I engaged in the lifestyle, the more constricting it felt. I was choosing friends, activities, books, movies, and places based on homosexuality. It was tiring and limiting. It felt ridiculous to be basing my life only on sexuality.

One other disturbing revelation was that I expressed my sexuality out of brokenness. I knew I was living this way because I had been deeply wounded. Even if it seemed that I had chosen this lifestyle because I wanted it, I knew that I had chosen it because I was too afraid to face what was really going on in my heart: idolatry, fear of men, insecurity, and feelings of worthlessness. I knew that I made the choice out of weakness, not out of feminist empowerment. I knew if I stayed in the gay lifestyle, I would be living half a life.

At that time, a friend told me about a ministry in Chicago that was devoted to discipleship. I decided to give God one more chance by spending two months there just putting myself in the ways of God. The people there told me the truth boldly, yet with great love, and I made the decision to trust God for my healing and restoration. I realized that this struggle was life or death for me. For me to be free, homosexuality had to symbolize death. The verse I memorized and wielded like a sword was Romans 8:6, "The mind of sinful man is death, but the mind controlled by the Spirit is life and peace" (NIV).

More than anything, I wanted life and peace. I understood that I would have to see every thing in my life in the light of that verse. I would have to ask, "Is this thought life or death to me? Is this person life or death to me?"

I got serious about working on the issues that were causing me to turn to women for comfort, approval, and completion. These issues included abandonment, anger, victimhood, emotional dependence, jealousy, fear, insecurity, idolatry, worship of the feminine, and a hatred of the masculine.

I sought counseling, received much prayer and support, and maintained my integrity by being honest about my struggles and confessing my sin. For a while, I coasted along by doing what was right outwardly. I held on to the thought that I could go back to my sin if being a Christian didn't work out. Then someone confronted me, saying that I had to give up the option of ever going back if I wanted to experience lasting, authentic healing and freedom.

It was hard to give up physical relations with women, but much harder to give up codependent relationships, masturbation, fantasy, and the idea that I was free to go back to my sin whenever I wanted. Once I realized that and saw the high cost of holy living, the real grief set in. I experienced a deep sense of loss. I knew I had to give up self to find God, but I didn't know it would be so painful to shed my identity and take on another.

I discovered that more than anything, I did want to honor God with my life. I came to know many other people who had struggled with life-dominating sins. They took a risk and told me their stories, giving me hope and a tangible example of the power of God manifested in his people. I wanted that for myself so I threw myself into getting healed. It's been a long, hard road with a bit of backtracking and meandering, but God has been so faithful and he's made me a person I never thought I could be. He really has given me hope and a future.

There have been times since then when I've been dangerously close to stumbling. I wasn't miraculously healed of all same-sex attraction. I continually have to guard my heart and mind against it. But it has nowhere near the same power over me that it did.

One of the most important elements in my healing was the presence of other people who would not let me give up. They were not afraid to talk about sexuality in general and homosexuality specifically. They knew that telling the truth in love was messy but persevered anyway. They began a dialogue with me and were consistent in their example, their prayers, and especially their own transparency.

When I was living in the ministry mentioned earlier, I most appreciated others willingness to share their stories with me. While my life had consisted of not telling the things I had done, their lives consisted of not only telling others what they had done, but more important, of sharing what God had done in them.

It has been said, "Confession breeds confession." If you want to be someone who people can talk to and confide in, you have to be no stranger to confession yourself. Make confession a lifestyle. Dietrich Bonhoeffer said simply, "Confession is discipleship."

At one time I didn't think I would make it to twenty-one. I truly believed there was no hope for me. But God pursued me relentlessly and drew me back to his side again and again, delivering me from bondage and despair. Nevertheless, this isn't the end of my story. When the Lord delivered me he also delivered me to a ministry of mentoring. I love walking alongside other women and being a part of their stories. Being involved in mentoring other women is a way for the Lord to bring glory to himself through my struggle. I don't have to walk in shame anymore, knowing that he has made all things new, including me!

Several years ago, the Lord also blessed me with a husband who has been an amazing example to me of the steadfast love of the Lord. At that same time, the Lord led me into women's ministry where I discovered a gift for walking alongside other women seeking wholeness and hope. God is a giver of good gifts, and he has even now blessed my husband and me with a daughter. I am still surprised that God would take my life and make it into a testimony of his faithfulness and extravagant love for the lost and broken.

7

Turning Points

William Harrington[10]

I was born and raised in Buffalo, New York, where I grew up in a broken family. Both of my parents were alcoholics. After they divorced when I was five, my mother was forced to take care of me and my three sisters alone. Because she also had to work full-time to make ends meet and provide the basics, we were pretty much left on our own and had little guidance.

The age of thirteen proved to be a turning point in my life. It was at that point I began to get involved in behaviors that held me captive for years. I began experimenting with alcohol and drugs and then, finally, homosexuality. I was taken to my first gay bar by someone who believed that the only way to deal with my confusion was to get me involved in the homosexual lifestyle. That was all I needed. It seemed so right. It opened a door for me.

Because I had always believed that I was born gay, this new world became the focus of my identity. I began to openly identify myself as a gay man and relate to everyone on this basis. I felt that I was born this way, that there was nothing I could do to change and that there was really no need to do so. This went on for ten years.

What I didn't know was that my mother was praying for me. She had become a Christian and was burdened by my lifestyle. A few years after her conversion, I agreed to speak with someone from her church, while visiting my family in Florida. This visit became a second turning point for me, because during that visit, I had a conversion experience and became a Christian. Somewhere

---

[10] Like Steve, William has gone to be with the Lord.

inside I knew that God was going to do something about the homosexuality. It had to be dealt with.

The Lord dealt with me in two phases. The first stage was in regard to alcohol and drugs. At that time they were so closely tied into my identity as a gay person that I had a hard time dividing the two. God gave me the motivation to get help through a twelve-step program. It was not easy! Those coping mechanisms were deeply ingrained. Still, I knew I was on my way out. But my sexuality would prove to be the most difficult issue of all.

I moved to Philadelphia, and my mother found out about Harvest USA, a ministry in the area that helped people leave the homosexual lifestyle. I knew that I didn't want to continue in the lifestyle, but felt paralyzed with fear. I rarely went out of my apartment because I was afraid I would encounter the wrong person or situation, not be able to handle it and give in.

I had many doubts about God dealing with my homosexuality. Was God really able to change this? It had been there for as long as I could remember. For my first three months in Philadelphia, I would just lie in bed and cry myself to sleep.

I knew that I was a Christian though, and had to have some type of support to deal with this. I gathered up my courage and began to go to the Harvest USA meetings. As I started to make connections with others trying to deal with homosexuality within a Christian framework, I began to get more confidence. Bit by bit, the Lord enabled me to come out of my shell of fear and doubt. My identity began to change.

The Harvest USA support group helped me to see what being a Christian man was about. I realized that I didn't know what a man was supposed to be! After all, I had grown up in a family with four women and had no experience to draw upon in learning how to be a man or what it meant to be masculine. During this time of growth the Lord showed me that I had been searching for a father figure all along to learn how to be a man. As I became involved in healthy, growing Christian relationships, I began to learn what a Christian man really was.

Today, the sense of fear and shame that I first experienced as a new Christian has nearly dissipated. Now I endure just the everyday struggles of growing as a believer, including struggles with temptation. My family has been very supportive. So has my church. The new relationships there have made it much easier to come out of the lifestyle.

Little did I know that God was placing all this support in my life for a reason. I've recently been diagnosed with AIDS. That's been hard to live with. Yet I know that God can use my testimony to show his mercy and faithfulness. It is difficult to think of death, but I've realized that as a Christian the worst outcome is actually the best outcome for me: eternity with God.

God has placed his hope in my life, and I'm becoming the man he created me to be. No more using other people to get my own needs met; no more hiding or shame. I am so thankful to the Lord. He's done more than I ever imagined.

In Memoriam

John Freeman

As his struggle with AIDS progressed, William became even bolder in his witness for Christ. He talked with others about his illness, his redemption in Christ and his future home in heaven. About two years after writing this testimony, William went to be with the Lord. After I received the call about his death, I immediately went to his home. Several of his closest friends gathered around his bed, where we just sang and prayed together.

Several days later three of us drove up to the Great Lakes area and participated in his memorial service and burial. William is greatly missed and made an indelible mark on our lives.

8

A Woman Under the Influence

Gwen[11]

Now that I stand back and look at my prior lesbian relationship I can see that the woman I was involved with gave me the love and attention I had long craved. I grew up liking to be alone and feeling that my own company was much better than the worry of someone else's. I didn't have to be concerned with getting on my own nerves, pestering others, or messing up anything. But deep inside I was longing for a woman to be deeply involved in my life.

The woman I was involved with was patient and kind. She was like a dream come true. She taught me things. For instance, I had always wanted to play softball and be on a team. She bought me my first glove and even got me on her team. I played for two years. On weekends, she would give me batting and catching practice. She also bought me a camera and taught me how to use it. We would go to parks, the zoo, or the forest and take pictures.

She taught me about life and about love. But she only taught me about one kind of love: a selfish kind. She needed to be needed by me as much as I needed her. Our relationship was far from healthy. It was focused on our selfish needs and we used each other to get our needs met.

She is no longer a part of my life.

In her place, I now have other women who teach me about a different kind of love. They teach me about Jesus' sacrificial love and love me with his kind of love. The way I act sometimes, I

---

[11] Gwen is a pseudonym.

am blessed they love me with Jesus' love. I have tested their love. I have tried to get myself kicked out of their lives, but as one of them said, looking at me over her glasses, "Honey, we are here to stay."

Sometimes you have to take risks. I fought against attending the Women's Support Group at HARVEST USA for a long time. My counselor must have known it was what I needed. Soon "I don't want to go" turned into "I don't want to leave."

After my arrival at HARVEST USA, I grew and developed in ways I never thought I would. To be honest, the group work was not always easy. At times it was tough, but worth every tear and frustration. I learned to develop healthy female relationships and to live as the woman God intends me to be.

I continue, years later, to have women teaching me that I can actually enjoy being a woman. These women are not prissy. They are not weak and fragile. In fact, a few of them remind me of my military father more than I wish. I am learning that women can be strong and capable, and still be feminine.

I'm learning how unpredictable the healing process can be. Here are a few examples: One woman at my church has the ability to give the best hugs you could ever want – and they are not in the least erotic. She is able to show an almost motherly affection without making me feel like a child. Another woman simply shows respect for my feelings. I am not accustomed to someone caring about how I feel. It is marvelous that a woman can care for me without having a lesbian agenda. Yet another woman is in a position to set down rules and guidelines for my life. This is something that has never happened before. After the initial shock of allowing her and others to speak into my life in healthy and definite ways, I can see how it is helping my healing process.

This variety of experiences is moving me closer to God. What I needed to break me free from my struggles with same-sex attraction was to be incorporated into a community of believers where the women became genuine friends and cared for me, showing me how to be the woman God wanted me to be.

If you are struggling as I was, I encourage you to take the first step to get help. Find a ministry like HARVEST USA. Give it a call[12] and make an appointment. I am sure someone will meet you at the door and you will begin the journey home. You can experience the love and power of God in your life.

---

[12] Go to the HARVEST USA website (www.harvestusa.org) for a list of our local offices. You can also go to www.exodusinternational.org for a list of related ministries.

9

A Reconstructed Life

Gordon[13]

I remember standing and singing a love song to my bride as she came down the aisle. Our dream had come true and we were joined as husband and wife. How was this possible for a former homosexual?

For Mary and me our marriage is a wonderful testimony to the power of God to transform lives. My change began when I first started seeking Jesus, wanting to come out of a lifestyle that had started out exciting, but over eight years had turned into a lonely, guilt-ridden existence.

My father was an alcoholic and our relationship was not good. At the age of seven, I lost my mother to cancer. This, and my father's alcoholism, tore apart what was left of our family. My mother's dying request had been for me to live with my older sister, and after my mother's death I left my father's house. Feeling as though I was never wanted, I made an early vow to "never be like my father."

As the years went by, I sensed a difference between myself and other boys. My interests were more toward the feminine, like playing with dolls and with girls rather than boys. I felt a deep inadequacy in relating to boys my own age. At an early age, I became sexually involved with a neighbor boy. Although, at the time I somehow knew this was not right, I desperately needed

[13] Gordon is yet another individual who has gone to be with the Lord. It is heart breaking how many of the individuals who share these testimonies have contracted HIV/AIDS as a result of their sexual activities. We thank the Lord that medical advances now offer a better prognosis for those who have contracted this disease.

his friendship and didn't want to lose him. As I grew up I became aware of an increased emotional and sexual attraction to men. I didn't understand these feelings and wanted them to stop, but they didn't. These unwanted feelings and being told I was a "fag" and "queer," left me confused and believing I was born that way.

About three years after high school graduation, I met a woman who shared the Gospel with me. I went home that night and asked Christ to come into my life. My feelings didn't change and for the next three years I struggled with my homosexuality, fearful of sharing this part of my life.

Deciding I could not take the hypocrisy anymore, I officially "came out" into the gay lifestyle. In the eight years that followed, I had several relationships with men and countless one-night stands. I became deeply involved in the gay community. Although on some level I was aware of anger toward God and guilt over my behavior, I tried to dull the feelings by drinking and using "party drugs." I know now I was looking for the father image I so desperately wanted.

Finally, I couldn't stand it anymore and was at the end of my rope. I cried out to the Lord one night to "help me get out of this lifestyle and set me free." Soon after that, a friend told me about HARVEST USA, a ministry for people wanting to come out of the lifestyle. Realizing that I had been in rebellion like the wayward son in Luke 15, I admitted, "Father, I have sinned against heaven and against you." In that parable, I also read these incredible words about the rebellious son's return: "But while he was still far off, his father saw him and was filled with compassion; he ran and put his arms around him and kissed him" (Luke 15:20, NRSV). With the promise of these truths, I came back to my Father.

Through the loving encouragement of other Christians eager to talk to me, pray with me, and spend time with me, the Lord began to work a change. At the HARVEST USA meetings, I learned some life-changing Scriptures and was given some well-written Christian books on homosexuality. The Lord began to heal me as I spent time with Jesus in prayer and in the Bible.

I also began attending a warm, caring church and going to a weekly home Bible study. There I met Mary. One night she began to share some burdens of her heart, and I felt the Lord telling me to give her a big hug. I did! During the following months, we began to form a friendship. Over two years, our friendship deepened into an undeniably romantic relationship.

In God's amazing plan, Mary had sensitivity for those coming from my background and had been volunteering in the office at Harvest USA before we met. Earlier in her life, she had studied to become a Dominican sister but felt led, after a year and a half, not to continue in the convent. Going through that painful time of frustration, anxiety, and emotional turmoil helped her identify more with my struggles. We both felt a deep sense of God being the author of our relationship, and we grew more deeply in love with each other and with the Lord. We became engaged and were married a year later.

Together, we have had times of struggle, but the Lord has always been there for us. We continue to have a strong sense of his presence and peace. The biggest trial we have had to deal with occurred two weeks after I asked Mary to marry me. It was confirmed that I had tested positive for HIV disease.

Although there have been times of fear and doubt, our faithful God had been right beside us. Gaining hope and comfort from God's word, we have sensed his moving forward with us, especially in regard to our marriage. We seek the Lord in prayer, reminding ourselves of what he says in Psalm 91:14b-15, "I will deliver him; I will set him on high, because he has known My name. He shall call upon Me, and I will answer him; I will be with him in trouble; I will deliver him and honor him" (NKJV). This Scripture has been my strength.

Our God is so merciful and loving. We want to serve the Lord and keep telling others that they can be free from the power of sin. I know that what I was looking for in other men, namely complete love and acceptance, can only be found in the Lord Jesus. The confusion that characterized the earlier years of my life, combined with a sense of rejection from other males, helped form my homosexuality. I know that in my case, homosexuality was a learned behavior and therefore, I can unlearn it as I grow closer to and more like Christ.

Our marriage is not proof of my freedom from homosexuality. It is one of the most beautiful blessings and fruits of the Lord's ongoing work in my life. "The Lord's loving kindnesses never cease, for His compassions never fail. They are new every morning; Great is His faithfulness" (Lamentations 3:23-24, NASB).

In Memoriam

John Freeman

It was an honor to be involved in Gordon and Mary's lives for over six years. I watched Gordon grow during those first years at HARVEST USA and then as a member of Tenth Presbyterian Church, where he and Mary were married and quite involved. Later they moved to New York City for several years where they worked for a large well-known street rescue mission, sharing the love of Christ. Gordon died of complications of AIDS about ten years ago. Mary lives in Center City Philadelphia and continues to serve Christ.

10

Becoming God's Man

Joe Pugh[14]

My childhood was typical of many men who struggle with homosexuality. My father and I were never close. He reserved his praise for my older brother, who was more masculine, tougher, and more independent than I was. If the truth be told, he was also harder working. I became used to their contempt. My brother had several friends who also found it amusing to belittle me. It didn't take long for me to conclude that those guys were not deserving of my efforts to please them. In particular, my father became the object of my contempt. Gradually other circumstances moved me to the unhappy conclusion that all fathers were insensitive and threatening.

Grade school and most of high school were an exercise of withdrawal. I usually earned good grades to keep Dad off my back, and to convince myself that I was good at something. But I avoided sports and social events like the plague. If I had any passion, it was religion. Brought up in Catholic school, I modeled myself after the priests who, I naïvely thought, didn't have much to do except say Mass and be nice. That sounded doable to me.

I kept well away from the main group of "normal" boys whose sports, crude sense of humor, and tendency to bend the rules all seemed contemptible to me. I had no idea that they were learning how to become men – albeit imperfectly – while I was learning nothing more than how to become a "nice guy." I saw the world

---

[14] Joe Pugh was a member of the HARVEST USA staff for several years keeping track of the finances. He also volunteered and helped with groups for men who struggled with same-sex attraction.

with no more clarity than if I were looking through stained glass windows during a rain. Even my stained glass image of Christ had become so wet that the colors were bleeding. The masculine Jesus of the Bible had become a gentle, non-threatening lamb. This emasculated Jesus became my role model.

I stayed in my religious cocoon through junior high and into high school, when my quiet snobbery and passive demeanor made me a target for the more overtly troubled kids. They needed a scapegoat and discovered I could be one. On school nights I went to bed with the standard high school insults ringing in my ears and a vow in my heart never to consider masculinity such as theirs as something worth pursuing. I, who had been rejected, came full circle and rejected many others.

The only saving grace I had entering my young adulthood was a genuine, if distorted, passion for a God who absolutely forbade homosexual acts. I knew that I could not seriously consider the gay lifestyle. Instead I became involved in young adult singles groups with an eye intent on gobbling up every ounce of attention I could from any male Christian. Every rejection from a Christian brother poured gasoline on the fire of "poor rejected me." Any affirmation or affection from a man encouraged me to believe that my relational patterns were legitimate. While I dated young women on and off, I always found an excuse to escape if the relationship seemed to be getting serious.

When my twenties drew on and my friends started to get married, I realized that I would not remain young forever. I began to seek the Lord for his plan for my life. When the desire for a wife and children became deeply enough planted in my heart, the Lord moved me to ask out the woman who would eventually become my wife. Kathy and I had been in ministry together, and much of our relational framework had already been put in place. She was not a stranger to me, so I felt some security in our pre-existing relationship. However, as soon as she consented to go out with me, I knew I had a problem. My same-sex issues would be a serious impediment to marriage if I didn't get help.

Having been told about Harvest USA by a Christian friend some years earlier, I finally went to a meeting. I found it encouraging, began to attend regularly, and realized how badly I needed to change. I discovered that the key issue was not whether I had slept around, but what was in my heart. I came to see that I was really no different than the men in the group who had been the most promiscuous. I learned how to repent of my arrogance, distorted perceptions and fear of true manhood. I came to forgive my father, my brother and my old peers.

Within a few months, I realized I needed to tell Kathy about my issues before we started talking commitment. I sat down with her and shared everything. On that evening an amazing thing happened, not only did she express her trust in God and in me, but I realized that, having received her acceptance and support, I now felt closer to her than ever before!

Even so, I had a crisis to go through before becoming married. In the eyes of my faith, everything looked like we were God's plan for one another, and his path of healing was clear. In the eyes of my flesh I was a failure of a man who couldn't hope to make a decent, let alone happy, husband. I confessed to the Lord, "Father, I'm not strong enough! I just don't have it in me to walk this path!"

Though I did not hear a voice, it was as if he said, "I understand, but can you hobble?"

In over fifteen years of marriage, I've hobbled many times, and too often I've fallen in my sinful nature. But whenever I've let Kathy down, God has all the more made it up to her from his abundant provision according to the full measure of his grace and kindness. And many times the Lord has surprised me by giving me the grace to be more of a husband, father, and man of God than I ever thought I could be. He has also given me the gift of three wonderful children and Kathy's unwavering support. The grace of God and the support of other believers in Christ have made it possible for me to repent of my attitudes and actions, to forgive others and to grow in many relationships, including genuine friendships with other men of God.

A skeptic might ask, "Has your orientation changed?"

To this question I would respond, "To a degree, yes, but much more than becoming a ladies' man. I'm now becoming God's man."

In the debate over change and orientation, the value of obedience is often lost. Change involves continual choices of obedience over a lifetime. In this process, we must never forget our assurance of grace and help from God. It would be well for strugglers confronted by the taunts of those who say they cannot change to recall the words of Shadrach, Meshach, and Abednego. When Nebuchadnezzar asked them who could deliver them from the furnace if they refused to bow down to his idol, he was questioning whether circumstances or faith would rule.

Shadrach, Meshach, and Abednego answered the king, "O Nebuchadnezzar, we have no need to present a defense to you in this matter. If our God whom we serve is able to deliver us from the furnace of blazing fire and out of your hand, O king, let him deliver us. But if not, be it known to you, O king, that we will not serve your gods and we will not worship the golden statue that you have set up" (Daniel 3:16-18, NRSV).

I am not concerned whether my so-called orientation ever totally changes. I have experienced significant change and I will strive, by God's grace, to be obedient when tempted. For many years I was deeply concerned about whether a man or a woman would turn my head, but now I have learned that as Psalm 3:3 says, "...you, O LORD, are a shield around me, my glory, and the one who lifts up my head," (NRSV). God is the one who lifts my head above selfish concerns to grow into the fullness of Christ.

11

A Firm Place to Stand

Jack Cook[15]

My life in homosexuality lasted twenty-three years. I never really wanted to be gay. I don't think that initially it was something I chose, but, rather, something I became aware of. I felt attracted to men long before I got involved in the lifestyle. I suppressed my feelings for years and hoped they would just go away. By the time I was twenty-six I knew my attractions were not a passing phase.

I moved to Center City Philly, just to "test" myself and find out if I really was gay. As a result, I was quickly drawn into the lifestyle. At first it felt like a fresh thrill. I actually felt quite free. To justify my decisions, I adopted a tolerant position on just about everything. It sounded really good and was the mindset of everyone I ran with in my new community. At times I thought about trying to change, but after a while I just resigned myself to being gay.

Surprisingly, the most distressful time of my life came when I began to be drawn to Jesus Christ. When I was in my mid-twenties a Christian co-worker shared Christ with me. I sensed I needed help and asked the Lord to save me. I began attending a church. My struggle with homosexuality, however, continued. I didn't know what to do. I prayed constantly. Nothing happened. At church no one seemed to talk about this. Disillusioned, I left the church and resumed my life in the gay community, where I found others who shared my disenchantment.

---

[15] Jack is another brother who is now experiencing the joy of his salvation in the presence of his beloved Savior.

Sixteen years later, I saw an article about HARVEST USA on the front page of a local paper. I was surprised that a ministry actually dealt with homosexuality. I was even more astonished to find that my old church, Tenth Presbyterian, now sponsored this new outreach.

I began attending a support group that addressed the issues I had wrestled with for so many years. In that group I found others like myself who had given up hope. But I was also inspired as I heard how some were finding freedom from the control of homosexuality. This became my new community. Through some initial one-to-one mentoring by staff and then by attending the group meetings, I slowly experienced internal changes.

For the first time, Jesus Christ and the word of God became real to me. His word became practical for my life and struggles. I was letting important spiritual truths into my heart, in a new way. I slowly came to see that the same Jesus who had shed his blood for me on the cross to take away my guilt and shame was the one who could be the source of my wholeness and healing. Jesus wanted to be intimately involved with me – struggles and all. In fact, he had already laid the foundation for it by his perfect sacrifice on my behalf. Now he wanted to do business with me.

Realizing that the Bible really did apply to the problem of homosexuality, and that my sin was no greater and required no different solution than any other sin, was a revelation. Knowing that Jesus died for me and truly loved me gave me the incentive to want to live for him. The Lord began to turn my life around. First, he gave me the desire to follow him and, then the will and the power to begin to obey. As a result the last nine years have been completely different from all that went on before.

Through the power of God, I have been able to discard many of the elements that had held my life together. Gone is the continuous comparing myself to other men, the cruising, the use of pornography, and the attending of gay clubs and social groups. A few months after I began to attend the HARVEST USA group, I was even able to move out and leave the man I had been living with for sixteen years. Although the nature of our relationship had to change, I still care for him. Occasionally, I have dinner with him, sharing what God is doing in my life and inviting him to consider knowing Christ.

All these changes did not happen in a vacuum. The void left by what I had discarded had to be filled and was by my relationship with Jesus Christ, by God's word, by a new and vital prayer life, and by a social life that revolved around other Christians. As my relationship with the Lord developed, my church attendance became regular and my time of worship was enriched. I actually joined Tenth Presbyterian Church and become very involved.

I now see the Lord working through so many aspects of my life. I have realized that he never had his hand off me, even in my rebellion. It has not been an easy walk, but he's enabled me to walk it.

A crucial element of God's work has involved gaining a new view of others and learning how relate to them, especially how to love others well. I've also learned that I need Christian friends. The more that I nurture good, healthy friendships with the Lord's people, the less insidious or overwhelming the temptations and tendency to look to others to fill me up. I've realized that I spent years in homosexuality extremely dependent on other people and using them. These new friendships have helped reinforce what God is doing in my life.

Although the changes have occurred late in my life (I came to HARVEST USA at age forty-eight), it is something for which I thank the Lord. Psalm 40:1-2 sums up what God had done for me: "I waited patiently for the LORD; And he inclined to me and heard my cry. He brought me up out of the pit of destruction, out of the miry clay, And he set my feet upon a rock, making my footsteps firm" (NASB).

In Memoriam

John Freeman

One morning, about three months after Jack had begun attending HARVEST USA's Bible study/support group, I saw a large pile of boxes and furniture by the curb outside the row house where we had our offices. I naturally thought that another tenant had moved and left these objects as trash. As I got closer to this mound, I noticed a note taped to the top. It said simply, "I believe what you're saying. – Jack."

Jack had been living with his male partner in a very dark, abusive relationship for just over sixteen years. Evidently, in the middle of the night, after having heard the truths of the Gospel in our group, the Lord had impressed on him the need to flee his living situation – right then. In obedience, Jack packed what he owned and deposited it on the steps of the one place that represented safety and a new beginning. We immediately had to find Jack a new home. He ended up living with a group of single men from Tenth Presbyterian Church. Over the next nine years, as the Gospel took root, Jack grew tremendously and became a different man.

He became a committed volunteer at HARVEST USA, accompanying me on many speaking trips and often sharing his testimony. He became a blessing and trophy of grace (and one of the best babysitters my three young children ever had). Nine years after Jack wrote this testimony he had a heart attack and went to be with the Lord. Several of his closest friends and I participated in his memorial service at Tenth Presbyterian Church in Philadelphia, where Jack was an active member.

12

Scenes of Grace

Sarah Lipp[16]

The Stage

My family of origin seemed generally harmless. I didn't have any major traumas, any events that were unpredictable per se, or any significant disruptions. I was raised in an evangelical Christian home and became a Christian at the early age of five. I cannot remember when I didn't believe and trust that Christ died on the cross for my sins. In an effort to do the right thing, my parents heavily enforced and taught the parenting methods and morality offered by a popular radio ministry.

I have older twin sisters, so my Dad lived in an all-girl household – even the dog was female. We went on family vacations every year. My parents came to all my sporting events and were very involved in my schooling. They fostered my creative side and encouraged my self-confidence and esteem. My sisters and I were very involved in our youth groups and went on every youth retreat. In high school, we were all involved in Young Life – even my parents joined in to host many Young Life events at our home. Scripture, God, morals, discipline, and discretion were all emphasized in my upbringing. I truly had wonderful parents who loved me deeply. Outwardly, things seemed ideal.

But as far back as I can remember, I was attracted to or had crushes on females. I could easily follow the popular culture

---

[16] Sarah Lipp currently serves the Mid-South office of Harvest USA as the Women's Ministry Coordinator. She works with women who struggle with sexual sins, as well as with wives of male strugglers. She has a degree from Westminster Seminary with a focus on counseling and is working on a Ph.D.

today and say I was born gay, but I know differently. Growing up, I was uncomfortable being a female, and identified with and felt comfortable in maleness. The way I felt in my body and the feelings I had for female peers were more consistent with those of a male. However, I was also attracted to males, and had many crushes on boys my age and was, from all appearances, "boy crazy" growing up. Yet as I grew older, my fantasies began to reflect my true desires.

My fantasy life began around age seven. I was drawn to other girls who had qualities I thought would meet my desire to be nurtured, admired, and looked up to. I wanted to be the most important thing in her life and for her to share an intimate and intense connection with me. I wanted to be able to trust her with everything and have her trust me totally in return. I deeply desired her to be the source of my comfort, my security, and my status. I wanted my comfort to be found in her mothering and nurturing. I wanted my security to be found in her loyalty and our intimate bond. I wanted to have status in her eyes by being her protector and source of strength, and ultimately the most important person in her life.

When adolescence began, my emotional fantasies became eroticized. Being sexual, I believed, would create the ultimate bond. I was attracted to girls that I saw as "softer" females, knowing I could have my desires met through them. In short, I wanted the type of female who would make me the top priority. I wanted a secure position in her eyes and heart where I would be safe.

Influences Behind the Curtain

How does one understand the seemingly polar opposite of my fantasy life and my "good Christian" upbringing? Here unspoken and not-so-obvious family dynamics provide a window to how my desires developed. While my father and mother both played major roles in shaping me, my father played a crucial role in my developing a more male identity.

My parents were a classic picture of a June and Ward Cleaver marriage – straight out of 1950s TV. My mother did not work outside the house, but was a stay-at-home mom. My father owned his own business in the DC Metro Area where we lived and was very successful. I understood their black and white marital roles early on. My dad's territory was the exterior of the house: the yard, the trash, and the cars. My mother's was the interior of the house: the kitchen, cooking, cleaning, and laundry. This hierarchical and patriarchal model of marriage functioned as the "biblical model" emphasized by the authority figures in my life. My father was openly dominant, superior, and truly "wore the pants." My mother was submissive, inferior, and rode my father's coat tails in all things.

The disparity in this became evident when my father began to teach his daughters. While he expected his wife to fit into his feminine model, a role she agreed to as biblical, he sent a different message to his daughters. He taught us to be strong, competitive, competent, confident, and thinking go-getters. We were to be self-sufficient, self-motivated, and superior. Of course, some of these attributes are not necessarily undesirable in and of themselves, but within the context of our black-and-white world, these traits felt male. To have these attributes was to be right, and right was identified with my father's role and gender. The male was strong, competitive, competent, and confident. The male was always right. By pushing his daughters into these roles, he inadvertently pushed me towards thinking myself better suited to be masculine.

Reinforcing this confusion, my father criticized and minimized the role of my mother, the value of her femininity, and any stereotypically female qualities she had. Though unspoken, it was very clearly believed and demonstrated that being male was better than being female. Better to be like Dad, not like Mom. My father never said this aloud, but his actions were louder than words. From my point of view, my dad's position was great:

Who wouldn't want to be the captain of the ship with all her needs met the way my wicked heart desired? I wanted his position and the status he held. Why shouldn't I seek out relationships the way he did?

As well, my parents blatantly shaped behaviors promoting my male identity. My father bought me an old-fashioned razor (without the blade) so I could shave my face with him on Saturday mornings. I was encouraged to play sports as a way to be assertive, bold, and even dominant. I had a toolbox and a wheelbarrow to help my dad on the weekends. I was my father's shadow. My dad and mom cultivated my behavior, interpreting it as that of "daddy's little girl." But inside I was identifying with my father's role, gender, and sin patterns.

My mother was a well-boundaried person who showed love by doing things such as cooking for me, doing my laundry, making my lunch, tucking me in, driving me around to practices. At a young age my mother taught me all too well the "dangers of men," and early experiences confirmed her words that men were usually after "one thing." I believed I should never trust or be vulnerable with a man, especially sexually. This belief that men were dangerous developed into an intense fear that my mother would abandon me and some male perpetrator would come take me away and do awful things to me.

In an effort to help me break away from her when I entered first grade, my mom thought it best to curb the amount of physical affection between the two of us. She wanted to help me mature and not be "clingy," but that broke any emotional bond we had. In reaction, I felt abandoned and rejected. I soon understood that seeking to be affirmed by physical affection was to be wrong, weak, and embarrassing to my mom in public situations. Inside, I developed an intense craving for the nurturing touch I had once felt.

The Drama Begins

The fantasy life that had begun at age seven became a reality in my freshman year of high school. I met Ruth, who fit perfectly into my fantasies, and soon we became inseparable best friends. My emotions were finally able to be unlocked. It was only a matter of time before our relationship became sexualized. I had finally met the female who would make me her everything, who would take care of me, nurture me, mother me, and admire me. This relationship lasted nine years; nine years of feeling intense pleasure connected with intense shame.

We hid our secret until our infatuation began to show at school. At the time I was attending a Christian high school, and from all appearances my parents thought I was on the right path. However, the school administration got wind of our relationship and confronted my parents, Ruth, and me. Ruth and I denied it as usual, but we couldn't deny some of the hard evidence: eyewitness accounts of us acting "a bit too close for comfort" on campus. Subsequently, I was expelled.

Later, in college, Ruth and I began the struggle of changing our behavior by going to Christian groups, getting involved in church, seeking out other friends, and even having boyfriends. We thought we could change our inner desires and motivations. Unfortunately, we were trying to change from the outside in. The relationship finally ended amid violent physical outbursts of rage and bitterness in an effort to change. Ending with Ruth was excruciating!

But my pattern of relating to women remained the same. I still became emotionally dependent and pushed the limits of emotional intimacy. Trying to convince myself these relationships were benign, I believed that I was cured of my terrible secret sins since I wasn't overtly sinning physically. Soon, however, I had again crossed all the lines.

I knew I was going to fall the moment I met her. When I saw her I felt like I was on a train and couldn't get off. The delusion of falling in love with the "right one" blinded me again. Internally, however, I was devastated. I realized I had not changed and my heart was still inclined towards attraction to women. I felt I was homosexual and could do nothing about it; yet I struggled because I believed in my heart it was wrong.

I was wearing myself out with this desperate craving for connection, belonging, comfort, and safety in the arms of a woman. Though being with women would temporarily meet my desires, the well of my heart always ran dry. I was ever searching and wanting. I kept looking for "the woman" who would finally complete me. I found temporary contentment and intimacy in each lesbian relationship, but my convictions would never let me truly rest or find peace.

I remember revealing my struggles to a friend named Mary. She was a woman of wisdom who listened well; she looked me in the eye and said, "Sarah, this isn't who you are."

I responded, "But it feels like who I am!"

How could it not be who I was? I had spent most of my life pursuing the perfect relationship with a woman. Was the bulk of my life a lie?

Mary's words stuck with me, and I knew they must be true if there was any hope for me to change – to ever be free. This insight began my journey out of my hopeless cycle. I began to realize that it was not a genetic predisposition, but a twisted desire, which was ultimately a sinful desire, that was the problem. My actions were sinful.

Although I had other unhealthy relationships with women as I have traveled this new pathway, I truly had made the decision to turn from my sin. Repentance is a choice as well as a journey.

The Real Conflict

Much to my amazement, I eventually ended up in seminary. When I was assigned a self-counseling project during a counseling course, I chose the issue of homosexual fantasies. I realized that if I really believed Mary's insight – "Sarah, this isn't who you are" – then I had to do more than simply stop engaging in sinful relationships. I was desperate for true change and not just behavior change. I used the project to dig into the deeper issues that fed my homosexual desires. Through individual counseling, classes, and this project, I began to see what was at the root of my homosexual desires and actions.

I realized that my heart was worshipping false gods – not the Lord Jesus Christ who I confessed to be my God and Savior.

During seminary I understood for the first time that behavioral change is not heart change. I needed a Savior to truly free me from my bondage to these idols. I was worshipping and manipulating others to worship with me. My functional idols were comfort, status, safety, and security. Anyone or anything that would fulfill these for me became my savior. These desires in and of themselves are not wrong, but I had made them into demands, requiring others to serve me. They became lusts – lusts for my own comfort, my own status, my own safety, and my own security. I worshipped created things (Romans 1:25) instead of the Creator. I worshipped women and how they could meet and fulfill my cravings (Romans 1:27).

The Resolution Takes Shape

In my heart I had been shaking my fist at God for not meeting my emotional demands and for allowing me to have this "abnormal" struggle of same-sex attraction. In my effort to be lord of my own life, I had become a slave to my desires, demands, cravings, and lusts. I manipulated others to serve me. In his mercy, God opened my eyes to show me that he is the only lasting source of comfort. Only by God's grace did I begin to see that true and lasting comfort, security, safety, and belonging are ultimately found in my relationship with Christ.

My parent's marriage now served as a mirror for my own heart. I saw that I had treated others, particularly women, the same way my father had treated my mother. I could see the depth of my need for the blood and grace of Christ Jesus. Seminary became sweet to me as I learned more and more of the depth of Christ's saving work. Ephesians 1-3 particularly became a joy and pleasure to study. It was sheer delight to hear and trust that God had chosen me before the foundations of the world – that I am his daughter whom he adopted because of Christ Jesus.

The Confessions of St. Augustine greatly encouraged me as I struggled to change and repent from my old life patterns. Augustine was a Christian in the fourth century who lived a sexually broken life. After his conversion to Christianity, he wrote his autobiography, being open about the depths of his sexual sin – and even his struggles after conversion. His struggles with lust were real, but God granted him victory. Augustine gave me words to express my repentance and to describe my struggle and the joy I now had in the Lord. I gleaned hope from knowing that one of the greatest theologians of the Christian faith had experienced struggles like mine and found freedom in Christ.

A New Story Arises

Today I am still confronted with temptations to find my comfort, security, status, and safety by my own means. But, because of my adoption into Christ's family, my temptations and struggles no longer define me. My name is no longer "homosexual" or "lesbian." By the power I have in Christ Jesus, I have the option of living free from the tyranny of these desires. By grace, my focus is being conformed so it serves God and others, rather than seeking to be served. The Lord has given me a fresh understanding of what it means to be a woman. I treasure the fact that my Father appointed me to be a woman and to reflect his image through my femininity. Scripture is the gauge of what it means to be a woman – not the society I live in. My femininity is found in seeking to be like Christ and reflecting him on earth.

Even though I have given much attention to my parents, they were not the only influences shaping my same-sex attractions. I love my parents deeply, and I am thankful for them in my life. I am blessed to have parents who believe in the saving power of Jesus Christ. My parents were positive role models for me in many ways, despite the way I responded to the negative things. Much has changed in their hearts individually and within their marriage since my formative years at home. The Lord has chosen the parents I have. Understanding my own sinfulness has enabled me to be more loving and gracious towards my parents.

Having tasted freedom in the grace of Christ Jesus, my living Lord and Savior, I now desperately want to share my ongoing story of repentance in an effort to be a living example of how sweet the grace of God is. Trained as a Christian counselor, I want to be used as a tool in the heart change of others struggling with same-sex attraction. My life and ongoing testimony are hard evidence of the true and real hope found only in Christ!

13

No Condemnation

Ben[17]

I was reared in a family with one brother and two sisters – all older than me. In our home, my mother was the nurturing one, and although I loved her dearly, I craved my father's love. He worked hard to provide for us and so was absent much of the time. When he was around, he was busy, tired, and easily angered. He rarely had time for me. His favorite saying was, "Go peddle your papers!" We shared no interests. Talking with him was always awkward. I'm not sure I ever really pleased him or made him proud.

I viewed my relationship with God in the same way. Although I desired him, I had little hope of having a relationship with him. He was unattainable. I tried to convince myself that if I was good and worked hard, one day I would be worthy of his love.

Raised in a small community, I attended a church within walking distance of my house. My mother, having accepted Christ three years before I was born, took her children to church every time the doors were open. Phrases like "three services to thrive" and "seven days without attending church makes one 'weak'" motivated us to attend regularly.

According to the pastor, our church faithfully preached the Gospel. I would love to know what he meant because the Gospel I have come to embrace was not what I saw. While I heard that salvation came through faith in Christ alone, what I saw blended with this truth was a performance-based Christianity that set

---

[17] Ben asked only his first name be used.

standards for a relationship with God that I knew I could never attain. I was never told that this was the reason that Jesus had taken my place on the cross.

I don't remember how young I was when I was first exposed to pornography. I doubt that it was very graphic, but I do remember it had a strong attraction. Then, as a teenager, one of my neighborhood friends showed me a hard-core porn magazine that he had stolen from his uncle's bedroom. This was the first time I had viewed sexual acts between men and women. I was instantly hooked. The images burned into my brain and ignited my fantasies. However, instead of imagining myself with women, I wanted to sexually please the men who used them.

Other than some curiosity-based sexual exploration in my early teen years, I never physically acted on my fantasies with men until after graduation from high school. I had opportunity, but feared crossing the line from thoughts to actions. When I was fifteen, that fear protected me when a man stopped me to ask directions.

The conversation quickly moved towards sex. It was obvious to both of us that I had become sexually aroused, and I wanted to climb into the car with him. But fear paralyzed me and helped me say, "No." I cannot explain why God protected me. I sat on a hill on the street where I had been accosted for two hours after he drove away, in hope that he would return. When I remember that day, I am overwhelmed by God's patient and undeserved kindness in protecting me.

When I turned eighteen, I started to cruise adult movie theater restrooms and interstate rest areas. Sometimes I was a voyeur, sometimes a participant. More than once on the news, I saw the places I frequented raided by police. But that never stopped me from going back.

At twenty-one, I was arrested for engaging in homosexual sex in an adult theater restroom. During the night I spent in jail, I prayed for forgiveness and swore I would never act out again. But it wasn't long until I took the same chances, and my desire for men grew stronger. I no longer just wanted to experience sex with a man; I wanted him to tell me that I was the best he had ever had. I didn't merely want to please him; I wanted him to worship me.

Oddly enough, I rarely had sex with the same man twice. I knew that what I was secretly doing was not pleasing to God. It was more than homosexuality; it was idolatry. I tried to stop repeatedly. I did not want this life for myself. I wanted real relationships with real people and with God. I wanted to be married and have a family. So I compartmentalized my same-sex struggles and lived the illusion of the socially acceptable Christian life.

I attended a Christian college in South Carolina. Upon graduation, I taught in a Christian school for four years. I married a Christian, and we served the Lord in our church. Together, we raised a son in a home where we tried to actively live out our faith.

On the outside my life appeared normal and fulfilled, but on the inside there was not one minute of rest from my struggle with sin and my frustrated desire for God's approval. For forty years I hid this part of my life from everyone; including my wife.

Before we were married, I tried to share my secret sin with my fiancée. Not being totally honest, I told her that I had sex with a man one time and assured her that this was in the past, never to be repeated.

I wanted to believe that what I told her was true, but it wasn't. I sneaked away to have anonymous sex in an adult bookstore just three weeks after we were married. Realizing that determination alone would not bring me victory, I became all the more unwavering in hiding the truth. I feared that being honest would cost me my wife, my family, my friends, my job, and any hope of having what I perceived to be a "normal" Christian life. Pornography and same-sex encounters continued to be very much part of my life throughout twenty-one years of marriage.

Over the years, I sat in Sunday school classes that discussed relevant topics like sinful addictions. I wanted to be honest about my struggles and free of them. I longed for others to walk along side of me and encourage me. But I didn't see anyone else struggling. Instead of facing my sin, I sat silently in pain, telling myself I just had to try harder. Loneliness and despair, however, drove me deeper into my sin patterns. I continued to hide the truth because I was convinced that no one would love me if they knew the truth. I feared rejection from other Christians more than I feared hell.

I also accepted the fear of disease. You would think that the death sentence that AIDS promised in the early 1980s would have been enough to frighten me into changing my behavior. However, my sinful patterns were stronger than my fear of AIDS, so I convinced myself I would just have to be more careful.

Praise God that I never became infected with HIV. However, I did contract chlamydeous and passed it along to my wife. I can't recall how I explained that one, but somehow it blew over. My secret was still "safe." Either that or my wife chose not to ask questions that might produce answers that she wasn't prepared to hear. My marital infidelity continued, as did the pain associated with guilt and shame.

I did seek help during those years. Twice I paid psychologists to hear my confession. Both were Christians. Neither was helpful. One told me that if I wore a rubber band around my wrist and snapped it every time I had a lustful thought, I would eventually associate pain with the thought. That would lead me to eventually stop acting out. It failed to produce the promised result.

The turning point finally came through tragedy. My wife died, having suffered twenty years with a disabling illness. My horrible grief magnified the pain of my guilt. I know it doesn't seem possible, but I loved my wife. I thought that God was punishing me by taking her. I know now this was not true. Perhaps he was protecting her from the potential consequences of my sin. In any case, God was demonstrating a "severe mercy." It was severe and painful, but merciful because he was using these horrific circumstances to draw me to himself. I was finally reaching the point where I had had enough of the struggle.

Over the next twenty months, the Lord continued to draw me to himself as I began to regularly call out for him to reveal himself to me and take away the pain. For a long time, my behaviors did not change. Still trying to self-medicate, I engaged in sex more frequently and took more sexual risks. But I did not stop praying.

Two years after my wife's death I learned from my church's new pastor, that my spiritual condition was far worse than I thought. I had always thought that homosexuality and pornography were the roots of my sin problem. However, even before he knew my secret, my pastor told me that I did not need to merely stop sinning, but to find rest from struggling. Such rest could only be found in the love of Jesus Christ.

One Sunday, my pastor preached on the man who came to Jesus with his demon-possessed son (Mark 9:14-29) for healing. When Jesus asked him if he believed Jesus could do the healing, the man replied, "I believe; help my unbelief" (Mark 9:24, ESV).

I was that man! I had believed in Jesus since I was five years old, but still thought that God's love was contingent on my behavior. I needed help to accept that I could never make myself righteous in God's eyes. I needed help to believe that God could love me in spite of my sin. I needed to believe that not only did Jesus suffer the punishment for sin that I deserved, but that God had also credited Jesus' sinless life to me. I needed help to believe that I was no longer an object of God's wrath, but a son in whom he delighted. I prayed for another nine months, meditating on various scriptures, and tearfully crying out, "Help me overcome my unbelief."

Finally, my desire to know God's love was so great that nothing else mattered. I lost all fear of rejection. A friendship had been growing between my pastor and me. I told him that I wanted to share something I had never revealed to anyone. After my confession, to my amazement, he did not turn from me in disgust, but told me that God loved me and he loved me. He showed me Romans 2:4 where Paul writes that God's kindness leads us to repent. Through my friend, I felt God's pleasure for the first time. I repented.

I identified with the adulterous woman who was publicly accused before Jesus (John 8:3-11). I know the Bible doesn't tell us this, but I think that when her sin was finally revealed, the guilt and pain was so great, she might have welcomed being stoned by her accusers. Instead, when Jesus said, "Let him who is without sin cast the first stone," her accusers walked away (John 8:7-9).

When I confessed to my pastor, I was waiting for the stones. Instead, my friend told me there was no more condemnation. Jesus, my Savior, had set me free at last.

Spiritual change doesn't take place in secret. Only when sins come to light are the lies of Satan exposed. Satan had told me that no one, even Jesus, could love me. But he lied. In addition to caring brothers and sisters at Harvest USA, Jesus proved his love to me through many other Christians who encouraged me with the Gospel. Among these were my children, my siblings, and my best friend of thirty years, who is like a brother. Satan told me that if any of them knew my heart, they would desert me. Instead – praise God – our relationships have grown deeper. I know I don't deserve any of this. I deserve everything that Satan told me. All I can say is that it is God's grace!

Two years after all this, another unexpected blessing came into my life. I was not searching for a wife, but God brought an incredible woman into my life, who has shown me more of the unconditional love of Christ than anyone on this earth.

After our first date, I knew that if there was to be a relationship, it needed to be built on mutual love and trust. Before our second date, I told her everything about my past and how God had been working; within three months we were married.

Four years later, I am still amazed that she can love me and trust me. Actually, it's more than trusting me; it's trusting God. She knows that there are times that I still struggle with guilt, still waiting for someone to throw the first stone. She knows there are temptations all around me, but she understands the power of the Gospel to change lives. She believes what the apostle Paul wrote, saying, "… that he who began a good work in you will bring it to completion at the day of Christ Jesus" (Philippians 1:6, ESV).

Recently, my wife and I were sightseeing while on vacation. As we walked, I found myself looking at some men on the street. Six years ago, this would have led to fantasizing and strategizing over how I could meet them. However, when I realized where my eyes were leading me, God's Spirit seemed to say, "Ben, I love you, and I love those men. Remember, those men bear my image, too. They do not exist to fulfill your selfish desires, but to reflect the glory of their Creator. They need me as much as you need me."

What a kind and loving rebuke from the Lord! In that moment, God did two things. First, his kindness led me to repent. Second, he led me to worship him and to pray that those men would know his love.

However, the Lord wasn't finished working. Within a few days, I began to sense an increasing conviction that I needed to share this with my wife. I was faced with a decision to minimize the sin and hide or to confess it and ask for forgiveness. I didn't want to hurt or disappoint her. However, relationships cannot flourish with closeted secrets. I was ashamed, but I had lived with secrets too long.

She calmly listened as I told her what had happened. She said that she didn't understand why I looked at the men, but what really hurt her was the fact that I hadn't shared this with her sooner. Together, we talked. We prayed. We cried.

I've always known that honesty is an important building block of a committed relationship. Sometimes it produces pain, but the Lord is showing me that loving my wife does not mean avoiding pain. Loving my wife means sharing the real Ben with all his weaknesses and failures.

That afternoon, the last thing that my wife said to me was that she loved me and forgave me. Although both of us were still hurting, I knew that was true. It was yet another picture of the way Jesus loves us.

Although I am thrilled to share how God has worked in my life, it has been a painful exercise to recall many of the events. At times I just want to forget the past; I want it to have never happened. Thankfully God is redeeming even the way I view the past. He is teaching me that my past is not about what I have done, but is part of a larger story revealing what he has done for all of us. He is not asking me to share my story, but to share Christ's story.

Christ's story is simple. He has changed places with me. On the cross, he received the full punishment from God that I truly deserved, then gave me his perfect record. I am learning to share this story with joy because I'm beginning to believe the Bible. It tells me I am not the man that I used to be. Second Corinthians 5:17 says, "Therefore, if any man is in Christ, he is a new creation. The old has passed away; behold, the new has come" (ESV).

Still it is not always easy to believe the wonderful truth of the Gospel. A few months ago, the Red Cross held a blood drive at work. My blood type, O negative, is always in demand. I could not donate blood, however, because the Red Cross will not accept blood from anyone who has ever had sex with another man. Although I appreciate their efforts to keep our nation's blood supply safe, in that moment all I could think about was my failure.

Praise God, however, who sent me a word of encouragement through a dear sister in Christ. Her e-mail reads as follows:

Dear brother,

I am praying that every time you see the symbol, an ad or the mention of the Red Cross (interesting logo!) that you will remember that the blood of Jesus has purified you from all sin and purified you from all unrighteousness (1 John 1:7, 9). In so doing God will take the accusations and discouragement that the evil one wants you to entertain and turn your heart to praise and worship instead.

I just got a call from the Red Cross this week asking me for my O blood, but I was "too busy" to respond. To honor God's work in cleansing your heart, I will make a point of giving blood this week.

To him be the glory!

Every day, I thank God for loving reminders of his love that has made me a new creation. Pornography and homosexuality no longer define me. My wife reminds me constantly that God is giving "back the years the locusts have eaten" (Joel 2:25).

In closing, I want to thank my heavenly Father, who has given me the relationship with him that I thought I would never have. Although Charles Wesley didn't know it, he wrote my story in his great hymn *And Can It Be*.

Long my imprisoned spirit lay,
Fast bound in sin and nature's night;
Thine eye diffused a quickening ray –
I woke, the dungeon flamed with light;
My chains fell off, my heart was free,
I rose, went forth, and followed Thee.

No condemnation now I dread;
Jesus, and all in Him, is mine;

Alive in Him, my living Head,
And clothed in righteousness divine,
Bold I approach th'eternal throne,
And claim the crown, through Christ my own

One day I will claim the crown, but it will not be because of anything I have done. The fact that "he rescued me because, he delighted in me" (Psalm 18:19, ESV) has freed me. He continues to free me from sin.

14

Beauty in Winter

Mark Hartzell[18]

The Early Soil

From the desolate, wintry places of my life, God has grown things of beauty. I have tasted much brokenness, but Christ has worked his saving grace in ways I could never have imagined a few years ago.

I was born into a family where the dynamics set the stage for much disruption in my early childhood. I was second of three boys, and my older brother was brain-damaged from birth. Scott's special needs placed much stress on my family, and I felt ignored in the shuffle to care for him.

My father, who was emotionally absent, unstable, and unpredictable, suffered from manic-depressive disorder. This was not diagnosed until I was a teen. Dad was prominent in the politics of our small town, so we were pressured to "keep up appearances" at all costs.

My mother tried her best to cope, but ended up overcompensating for Dad's shortcomings by falling into manipulative and over-controlling relational patterns to hold our home together. She was a classic enabler, covering Dad's tracks and making excuses for his tirades and workaholic patterns in the family business.

---

[18] Mark Hartzell served with Harvest USA from 1998 to 2008 and was instrumental in establishing the Harvest USA Mid-South office.

I now recognize that I had a hole in my heart at a young age. I longed for real intimacy – especially male affirmation, identification, and affection. I remember the cycles of masturbation as early as age four or five, during naptime. I suppose I did it just to relieve the pain and stress and to provide a temporary sense of pleasure or comfort amidst the loneliness. It took me a long time to realize how that emotional deprivation and those compulsive behaviors had scarred me early on.

At age seven or eight, I discovered pornography. Dad kept a secret stash at home, but it was also passed around among his friends with a wink and a nod. It was heterosexual porn much like the fifties-style pinups he kept on the wall of the men's room at his store. But the exposure seared my heart. Was this what manhood was really about?

Around that time I developed some "feminine" habits and interests, hating the sort of maleness I saw in my father. With no one to encourage my involvement in any team sports, I became increasingly isolated from my peers.

Then the hormones of adolescence hit. I regularly crept to Dad's porn stash and an addiction to sexual gratification consumed me. Many days, I could think of little else during school. In my fantasy world, my hunger for male connection and intimacy became sexualized. Heterosexual porn was no longer enough, so I began to steep myself in homosexual magazines. I had an interest in women and started dating, yet deep down wondered why I had such twisted cravings.

Shame and anxiety plagued me even as I pushed myself to excel at school. I chewed my fingernails incessantly, but otherwise was a "good kid." I loathed the labels homosexual and gay. When taunts of "faggot" were tossed around the schoolyard, I always feared I had been discovered.

I think the fear of exposure – what the Bible calls the "fear of man" – was the only thing that kept me from acting out with another male, though I came close numerous times. Thankfully, no one actually propositioned me until college, when I was more grounded in Christ. During my early and mid-teens, I was torn with so much gender confusion that I would have been an easy target for a sexual predator.

A Fresh Start

Though we were a church-going family, I didn't really understand much about the Gospel until about age fifteen. Our church seemed little more than a country club with God as a cosmic Santa Claus somewhere far off. Then, just as I received some Christian books from a neighbor, I met people who were really different. They were college students who had started an outreach in my high school, and some of them showed me a love and concern I'd never tasted before.

I got involved in a Bible study, and devoured the Word. I entered into fresh, healthy friendships. Even though I looked respectable, I realized that I was just as big a sinner as the other teens in my school who used drugs or alcohol to cover their pain and make life bearable. On a weekend retreat, I embraced Christ as Savior and Lord, entrusting all I knew of myself to all I knew of him. Some big changes began because I had a new spiritual nature (2 Corinthians 5:17).

Yet my old sinful nature, my flesh, was by no means gone (Romans 7). Indeed it would take me many years to untwist the knots I had fashioned and to understand the Gospel's power more fully.

A Double Life

In college, I joined a vibrant campus ministry group. My growth in grace was real, and I served in numerous leadership roles, evangelizing and discipling others. I knew homosexuality was wrong, biblically and instinctively, but I still returned there in my fantasy life when things got tough. There were periods of "victory" over my flesh, yet I also fell back into addictive patterns as well. I expected the mess would go away on its own if I were just holy enough.

Why talk about it? No one needed to know.

Silence, however, encouraged the struggle to continue.

When my roommate discovered the gay porn I had forgotten to hide, I lied immediately and said I had found it in the hallway. I remember vowing repeatedly never to go back to porn every time I watched it burn in the hallway incinerator of my dorm. But as a dog returns to its vomit (Proverbs 26:11), I would eventually drift back when under stress.

I threw myself into academic achievement as a self-protective maneuver. My deceptions worked well. I could fool anyone and was secretly quite proud of that. In dating women I covered over my inner turmoil so well that I almost fooled myself.

I flirted with risky behavior, but always managed to escape sexual contact with another person. One time, however, I went to an adult bookstore, filled with so much anger that I considered taking the next step into the gay lifestyle.[19] A man noticed me, and I began to think about pursuing him. Of course, I would only attempt it if I knew I could maintain secrecy about my double life.

---

[19] Anger is a common motivation for both homosexual and heterosexual individuals to act out sexually. Anger is rooted in our wanting what we want when we want it and in having our desires denied (see James 4:1-4). I have never met a man who uses pornography who is not also angry about life. – Editor

Suddenly, another guy in the store recognized me and called out my name. It turned out our parents were good friends back in my hometown thirty miles away. In his drunken stupor, he kept on chortling and yelled, "Boy, Mark, what would our mothers say if they saw us here?" My cover was blown! The terror of discovery and loss of reputation jolted me back to myself. I turned and fled, but the first man evidently had more interest in me than I had in him. He followed me out. A high-speed chase ensued at 90 to 100 mph, weaving around cars on twisty, country roads.

Somehow I had eluded him by the time I skidded into a parking lot on campus and raced inside to the safety of a crowded dorm. The thrill was more than I had bargained for that time. I was scared away from acting out with another man. Looking back, it was God – and only God – who spared me from further scarring and even greater consequences of my sin.

Love and Marriage

I met Linda during my college years, and we became good friends. I was thrilled at the prospect of marrying my best friend. We married while I was at seminary. I truly loved Linda, and from her I learned much of what God intended biblical intimacy to be like. After a rocky start, we developed a fairly "normal" sex life and started a family.

It wasn't that I was seeking a trophy wife to prove that I was straight, but I did make the mistake of assuming my homosexual temptations would die out if I worked hard enough at sexual relations with Linda. Even though I loved her intensely, I couldn't bear to tell her all that was in my heart – the risk of rejection still seemed too great. "And maybe I don't ever have to tell her," I rationalized, "It would just hurt her anyway."

After a brief period in pastoral ministry, we moved to Philadelphia and I found a fulfilling secular job that enabled me to serve as an elder in our church. During this time, we were blessed to come into contact with teaching drenched in grace and to learn that Christians are adopted children of God. God loves us not because of what we do, but because of Christ alone. The Gospel was starting to sink deeper into my heart, and I was coming alive to the joy of living as an adopted son of the King of heaven.

The church God placed us in was Gospel-saturated. The other elders were men of transparency and surprising vulnerability; healthy male intimacy seeped into my life almost without my realizing it. They demonstrated what walking in ongoing faith and repentance looked like.

I came close to revealing the war within me as many of these men were candid about their own struggles with lust. I learned from them and from others to deal in an ongoing way with my pride, fear, and unbelief. As a result, my addiction to porn was controlled for longer periods. But when stress or disruption in my relations with Linda occurred, I would often retreat to my private world of porn and masturbation – even though I loathed it.

I easily justified my sin as not really damaging Linda, myself, or others. In my saner moments, I prayed that this terrible craving would cease, but I still didn't dare breathe a word of it. I suffered in silence and loneliness. I feared the labels gay or bisexual. I hated the lies and was miserable with all the pretending, but saw no way out.

God Breaks In

Then God, in his severe mercy, turned my world upside down. In a relatively short period, a series of crises occurred. I faced repeated surgery for hernia repairs that revealed the reality of the aging process. In addition, they were a reminder of my own brokenness and the wages of sin. Then Linda and I had to face the death of our third child by miscarriage. There was also the loss of a job promotion that I very much wanted. It seemed like my dreams were dying all around me.

In the midst this, God brought home to me the harm I had done to Linda and our marriage. I was an adulterer at heart, and couldn't stand the deceptions any longer. I told Linda everything, preparing for the worst. To my amazement, she responded with overwhelming grace and understanding, even through her shock and grief. Though the months ahead were difficult, I was experiencing Gospel freedom in a new way.

There then came the final loss, which God had been preparing me for. My Dad was diagnosed with terminal cancer and given two months to live. I knew that now was the time to forgive him and pursue him in a deeper way. I made the long trip to see him as often as I could, and the Lord kept me safe on the road even though my eyes often overflowed with tears.

I was surprised by joy as Christ enabled me to move toward and love Dad – even as his body and world fell apart. Then, wonder of wonders, God used me to lead Dad to a saving profession of faith in Christ, one week before his death. This overwhelmed me, especially after seeing no fruit in twenty years of praying for him.

I realized that my life would never be the same. All of these losses were having their redemptive effect on my cold, stony heart.

Through the Door

Even before Dad's diagnosis, I had finally come to the place where I didn't care who knew what about my involvement with homosexuality. Having known about HARVEST USA almost from its inception, I knew I needed to go there no matter what the cost. Linda supported me. For a long time I had feared attending the men's support group, but that fear finally melted away.

A pastor I knew, Jack Miller,[20] had this motto: "The worst you can think about me is only half the truth." His motto became mine. Even so, the first few times I attended the men's group were scary. I was overwhelmed by the honesty of these men, but exhilarated as well. The joy and freedom of the Gospel was once again refreshing my dry, hardened heart. As God showed me how much I had in common with them, my walls of isolation crumbled. Deep, healthy, male intimacy replaced the destructive, false intimacy I had been addicted to. Those Wednesday night meetings became the high point of my week. The accountability of those brothers became a lifeline for me.

Eventually, I was asked to be a volunteer leader of the group. I was delighted further to see God use the shame and pain of my life to point other men to Jesus.

Today… and Tomorrow

Though far from perfect, my life is different now in many major ways. I have a firm identity in Christ as a forgiven son, not an orphan. Porn's stranglehold on me is broken, and the freedom is deep and delightful. I know my own heart better, and I know Christ better. I know the warning signs of impending sin and heed them now. Accountability with other men is a significant part of my life. I can enjoy real, healthy intimacy with men and women because I am committed to forsaking my patterns of deception. I am committed to walking in the light of the Truth.

---

[20] Jack Miller was the founding pastor of New Life Presbyterian Church in Glenside, PA, and author of several books. His influence led to the creation of World Harvest Mission, which also publishes Sonship and Transforming Grace materials. – Editor

Yes, temptation still occurs, and will until I reach heaven, but the pull is much weakened and the addictive power of porn has been shattered. Repentance for sin occurs more quickly. My anger is better placed now; it is anger at sin and its effects. Forgiven much, I now love much.

Linda also learned to work through her issues as a wife of someone who struggles with same-sex attraction. She received help from one of the godly women on HARVEST USA's staff. Our marriage intimacy has never been sweeter. My children, I trust, now have the benefit of a father who seeks to be the head repenter in our household. The power of the cross has transformed and is transforming me and my household.

Over the more recent years, one of my deepest joys has been to minister with men who struggle with sexual sins and to help lead biblically based support groups. Amazingly, God is using things in my life that I thought were only going to be sources of pain and shame to bless others. I have found joy ministering to other men, out of my own experience, because Christ doesn't want me to waste my pain! I have a growing passion to see Christ exalted in our sexually broken world. In my life I see the truth of the words uttered by Joseph in Genesis 50:20 – events and circumstances that others meant for evil, God meant for good and the saving of many lives.

Christ has broken into the cycles of guilt and shame in my life. Homosexuality no longer defines me. Jesus Christ does. My life is now hidden with Christ in God (Colossians 3:2-3). He has given me his beauty for my ashes (Isaiah 61:3), and has caused healing waters to flow from the wintry deadness of my past. All praise and honor to him!

15

Surprised by Grace

Rich Yates[21]

Unexpected Consequence: Vengeance

I wasn't born gay.

I was born – like you – into a fallen world as a rebellious sinner at war with his Creator. I had no control over the environment or family into which I was born. That was God's decision. He is the Sovereign One.

The beginning of my life, as I remember it, is a recollection that begins somewhere around age five. Prior history of my existence is confirmed by others and endorsed by a few faded black and white photos. That history is part of me, but it is the memories I have held, the beliefs I have adopted, and the ways I have interpreted my history, that most likely have shaped who I became.

I was born the second of a set of twin boys, the third son of a post-World War II naval family. Dad wasn't home for my arrival. In time, I began to question if he didn't love his life on the ship more than he loved life at home with us. But Mom – she was always there – always home and ready to protect, feed, and teach us. She was my model growing up. I wanted to be like her in character. I saw her as a survivor, a sustainer, and a saint worth following.

---

[21] Rich Yates served with HARVEST USA from 1999 to 2005. A gifted speaker and counselor, Rich ministered with men who struggled with same-sex attraction. He and his wife Andrea continue to minister to individuals in need.

I was raised to believe God existed, but I didn't learn much about how my heart and mind could work together in rebellion against this good God. Nor did I understand how the desires of my heart were grounded in ungodliness.

By the age of five, I had concluded I was different from my twin and older brother. They seemed more alike than my twin and me. Each was right-handed, brown haired, and handsome. They tanned in the summer and played outdoors while laughing through their perfect smiles. In contrast, I was a pale, redheaded, left-handed boy with separated front teeth. I stayed indoors helping Mom with the babies while pondering the uncertainties of myself.

I adopted my brothers' taunts as truths that proved I was different and didn't belong to the family. I projected my lower lip into a pout, and withdrew into a fantasy world. The question forming in my consciousness was, "Who am I, anyway?" The fear of finding out began to terrorize me. Fantasy seemed a safer place than reality. In fantasy I could escape the pain of feeling different and rejected. It hurt to believe I was not like my brothers.

In hope of finding an identity, I looked to Mom. I gave myself over to pleasing Mom so that I might earn acceptance and a sense of belonging. I traded the playground for the house and my brothers' approval for my mother's. I stopped trying to win their affections. I choose to endure their insults in exchange for the glory of being Mom's right hand. I found a place of power within the family structure. From there I executed my self-defense tactics. My interactions with my twin and older brother grew into daily conflict. My resentment, envy, and fear of them as males mingled with my pride and determination to survive without them. In time, despite the shame and pain of it, I had learned to find pride in being perceived as different, as "Momma's boy." I decided I would hate what they loved and love what they hated. I would not be like them. I would be "Me."

I remember my desire for vengeance and retaliation. I detached from my brothers, and eventually others like them, and retreated further into my fantasy life hoping to create a world in which I could avoid the pain of their rejection – and gain the glory I so desired.

Unexpected Father: Rejection

By the age of five, I had also adopted the perspective from which I would evaluate my father. I adopted this position after surviving an encounter with him and interpreting his reaction as condemnation of me. My heart's longing and idealization of my father had collided with the reality of that man.

I missed my daddy for a long time – longed for him and fantasized about how delighted he would be to be home with us and me. I anticipated a loving voice and a welcoming countenance. But the man who entered our home appeared nothing like the one I had created in my mind. This man had a beard and a bark. He wasn't the clean-shaven, soft-spoken image that I sought. Startled, I ran behind Mom. He commanded me to come forward. In terror, I fled out the door. His voice, with the tone of an uncompromising authority, sounded behind me. He pursued me, caught my pale frame, and taught me to never again run away from him or disobey his command. Barking his rules while enforcing his power with strong and unfamiliar hands, his judgment shattered my fantasy.

A father's words, like a brother's, have the power to curse or to bless. They can sear the soul and brand the consciousness with a mark that never fades. And so it was. The first words I remember from my father caused fear and then shame. I choose to detach from him as I had from my brothers who continued growing as boys should while I grew into Mom's helper. Dad remained on duty somewhere apart from us. I rarely played. I helped around the house or went to school content with being regarded by my mom as good and responsible.

When I entered fifth grade, my mother insisted that my father retire from active duty and come home to help raise us. From that point forward living at home meant living "under my father's roof." His entry into our daily lives imposed a paradigm shift that altered the family structure. His words and male authority hovered with a militaristic expectation. The disciplinarian moved in and I increasingly resisted his demands. I stayed away from the house more and more. I sought a refuge away from the fighting, bickering, and tension. I dreamed of a life where I could have peace, acceptance, and love.

We went to a non-denominational church when my father joined our civilian life. The teaching was selectively biblical, centering mostly on sin, law, and punishment. Dad seemed to agree with this moral code, as had his father. "Spare the rod; spoil the child" seemed more their interpretation of Christ's Gospel then the grace of God that draws sinners to repentance with kindness and encouragement. I tried to be a good Christian, and I knew if my performance fell short I would go to hell. I realized I must perform to win approval, respect, love, and now forgiveness. Nonetheless, I was aware of a growing evil in me. I was filling with hatred for who I was and envy for who I wasn't. I was growing angry and bitter, and looking for a permanent escape.

Unexpected Teacher: Seduction

During my sophomore year in high school, an escape lured my dissatisfied and demanding heart. It appeared, to my surprise, in the face of a man who defied my understanding of men. Here was a man different from Dad or my brothers – he was gentle, soft-spoken and warm towards me. He invited me into conversation. He told me of his world of teaching, ballet, music, and artist friends. I told him about my family, thoughts, hurts, and fears. He listened and encouraged me to confide in him. My imagination was fired by his descriptions. It finally seemed possible to have a fantasy come to life. It sounded wonderful, better than any world I had ever imagined. It made my reality appear even more drab and deadening. I longed to know his world.

My debut into that world occurred in the winter of my fifteenth birthday. On a snowy evening, he escorted me to the Academy of Music to see Swan Lake. I was so excited! I had never been to the theater. Hundreds of sophisticated people were there. I felt special and elite. I delighted in finally being in an atmosphere where I could breathe freely. Here, fantasy was alive. Glitter and lights adorned a passing array of beautiful faces set on pleasure. There was no way I could have detected that all this was but a prelude to rape. After the ballet, my teacher called my parents and suggested I stay with him for the night since the roads were unsafe. They agreed, not suspecting he would unleash his lust on their son before the dawn.

But he did.

Sunrise witnessed my tear-stained face attempting to resume its self-protective mask of stoicism as my teacher cautioned me to keep our secret. He explained to me the "truth" that I was gay like him. He promised to help me, but said I needed to keep our special relationship under cover. I didn't believe I had any choice. I surely couldn't tell Mom about this. Sex was a taboo topic in our house. I didn't know what "gay" was. But words have power. They can bless or curse, especially when delivered by those to whom we look for love and acceptance.

Soon afterwards, I was sitting in our Sunday morning church service listening to the minister teach about sin and its punishments, when he mentioned homosexuality. I paled as he ranted how a man who has lain with another man is going to hell. I heard my sentencing: I was a homosexual going to hell. I swallowed hard as the truth of my sentence weighed upon my consciousness. Internal accusations, collected from over the years, massed together to riot against my hope that maybe I didn't have to be gay. The conclusion seemed inevitable. The accusations mocked my grasping for normalcy – for a piece of truth that might save me from the sentencing of "queer" – but there seemed no evidence to claim my innocence. Hadn't I always been different? Didn't I disappoint my father by wanting to be an artist instead of a sailor? Didn't I think more like a girl than a man? Wasn't it obvious to Mr. D what I wanted? The name seemed accurate; the sentence just.

I was a homosexual.

Satan was delighted with my conclusion – but God's jealousy was aroused.

Unexpected Conclusion: Homosexual

The conclusion I came to at age fifteen – that I must be a homosexual – did not alter God's truth. And when God's love is fired to jealousy, his redemptive interventions can melt and transform a sinful heart frozen by fear, anger, and abuse or they can allow the heart to become encased in icy unbelief. In my case, he chose the latter. He patiently waited until my pride could no longer warm my delusions or find an escape in burning affairs of the heart. I wintered in my frozen condition.

Armed for self-survival, I held two basic assumptions: (1) I was a homosexual, and (2) God hated faggots. To be homosexual in the '60s wasn't cool or chic – it was painful, shaming, and possibly evidence of some cosmic curse. The psychological community recognized homosexuality as a sexual deviancy, classifying it as an abnormal psychological disorder. "Queer," "faggot," and "sissy" were taunts used to tear into the minds of people like me. Nothing was safe and no one could be trusted. I believed it necessary to hide my "gay" identity.

The source of my shame – my "sexual deviancy," my gay identity – fostered an ironic pride, which, blended with shame, filtered all my understanding. Enemies seemed to lurk everywhere. Comfort and temporary relief from existing in a hostile world was increasingly linked to sexual release. The "forbidden" of sexual sin, its implied danger and tantalizing invitation to risk, stimulated my adrenalin. Sin granted a momentary surge of forgetfulness blending risk, shame, pleasure, and condemnation into an explosion of sensual fireworks – in that moment I could separate from the reality of me and believe my heart was free.

My schoolteacher's flattery and seductive promises transformed into demands that I meet his needs and conform to his standard. He pointed out my flaws; my legs weren't as muscular as he would like and my social skills needed improvement. My value seemed only in serving his lust, which I tried to do even though it continued to assault me with a sense of condemnation. Afterwards, he would send me home on the subway alone and questioning, "Will I ever be enough?"

When I was sixteen, he took me to my first gay restaurant in Philadelphia, where he introduced me to the subterranean world of darkened interiors and lurking glances. In a smoky, dimly lit corridor, an exotic but strangely sad hostess greeted us with a dark smile. With a sly wink, she took my coat. I wondered who she was.

The ambiance was that of a hidden, soiled intimacy. While we were reading the menu, a waiter stopped and told us that another man had sent me a yellow rose and wished to buy us drinks. My lover responded with a passionate, "No!" Questioning his vehement reaction, I looked about to see the mystery man. I was awakened by the fact that someone here had sent me a rose. Someone here desired me, found me attractive, and wanted me.

My teacher had lied when he told me I needed him because there were so few like us. In fact, there were many like us here, and he was holding me for himself. My anger swelled along with a new sense of perverted pride and power. I threatened him. I said if he ever touched me again I'd tell everyone all he had done to me. Unholy passions for something and someone new flooded my heart. A fresh fantasy, fed by the lurid suggestion encompassed in that rose, was unleashed. I could know the "love" of many. The temptation to power, pleasure, and escape from pain lay next to my menu in the form of that yellow rose. Pushing down a conscious warning, I foolishly swallowed the bait hoping to find contentment in the promise of a mystery man seated in the darkness of this uncharted universe.

Unexpected Emptiness: Yellow Roses

The decades between swallowing this heady bait and my forty-second year were full of disappointment and disillusionment. My search for warmth and real love continued. I continually sought a fresh yellow rose to rekindle my hope. I struggled to survive the coldness of life in a fallen world. I tried to discern truths from lies and evil from good, but could not. I was not only cold, but also blindly groping to find a safe fire where I knew I was desired and acceptable.

Being drafted to Vietnam and seeing fellow soldiers die all around me, did nothing to soften my heart. Indeed, I became further entrenched in my self-protective, survival tactics, realizing that friends I cared about could die and be taken from me at any time.

After returning from Vietnam, I vacillated between trusting no one and desperately seeking someone to trust. Each new lover was eventually exposed as a fallen man like me. As we gave ourselves to deeply twisted sexual acts, we would shrivel up inside. Our sexual passion for each other eventually burned out. My hope for salvation in them was extinguished by their inability to fix me. I was like a brute beast, inflamed with passions and warring against all who attempted to quench them. I thought it better to live in a sexual cycle of pain, seduction, gratification, and guilt than to fall defeated by admitting my inadequacy and crying out for help.

I knew worldly success, however. Though I never followed through on the art scholarship I had won years before, my creative skills brought me a lucrative job in the fast-paced world of fashion design. I grew accustomed to the perks of this high-tension world: the trips to exotic destinations, plump expense accounts, lavish dinner parties, a condo in Manhattan, and a beach house in a plush Long Island enclave. But the Mercedes-Benz, the yacht, and all the fine crystal – even the heavy doses of alcohol and nicotine – couldn't tame the gnawing pain. The yellow roses kept fading, but I kept trying to find fresh ones – for twenty-five years.

Unexpected Intervention: God's Grace

Then, suddenly, God bombarded my frozen heart with a blazing attack. My father was involved in a near-fatal car crash, which forced me to confront a dreadful reality: I had never told my father I loved him, and I wanted (needed!) to hear him tell me he loved me. But my lover of nearly seven years didn't want me to go. We were beyond the fantasy of expecting to fulfill each other's dreams, but were emotionally enmeshed and resigned to one another. We were monogamous, yet empty within. Our arrangement seemed as adequate as one could realistically expect. But as my father lay in a hospital near Philadelphia fighting for his life, my lover and I quarreled over whether I should stay in New York for the christening of our new (and, of course, larger) sailboat or return to my father's bedside and wait for a better prognosis than death.

"Why's it so important to be next to your father," he prodded, "What did he ever do for you? Your being there won't change anything."

Stunned at his hard heart, I angrily stormed out of town. Stubbornly, he launched the boat solo. Two determined men each chose their own way.

On Sunday, when I returned to New York, the phone was ringing as I entered our condo. I heard the hysterical crying of my lover's sister. "It's Stan," she croaked, between sobs, "something horrible has happened! The Coast Guard found him alone on the new boat in Long Island Sound. He was unconscious…they think he's had a stroke."

I paled as her words sank in. First my father, now my lover… My world heaved downward in a trough of despair. I lost my mooring of self-sufficiency. For the first time I could remember in twenty-five years, I cried out to God: "Why are you doing this to me? What did I do?"

I shuttled, for the next eight months, between two rehab centers in two cities, watching the two most important men in my life fight to hold onto life. It was sobering to sit by them and realize their mutual finiteness; how they needed divine intervention. Then I began to realize I did too. Severe mercy awakened me and called me to turn back to God. God's love began to defrost the edges of my frozen heart.

That Easter Sunday, I wandered into a church in Manhattan. I needed to confront the Awesome Power that changed lives and caused mortals to ask questions they want so much to avoid. When the minister spoke from the pulpit, I was shaken into reconsidering one of my assumptions. He invited the congregation to join him in his delight to have Jim with them that day. Jim was an AIDS patient from St. Vincent's hospital. I was shocked and perplexed. These Christians were welcoming a homosexual into the warmth of their house. They didn't throw slurs, and they told him how God loved him. Were my assumptions false? How many other false assumptions might I be dying under?

Night after night, I sat alone in our condo sipping vodka martinis and smoking Marlboros, thinking about men suffering in rehab centers and questioning my assumptions, while reading the Bible that my lover's mother had given me at the hospital. For the first time, the TV was off in our place, and I quietly sat, with my cocktails, my cigarettes, and the Bible. Little did I know my own rehabilitation had begun.

In the wilderness of my isolation, the Holy Spirit used his word to minister to me, bringing warmth to my soul and a breath of reviving hope. The Spirit of God sat with me during those months of watching Dad and my friend regain a semblance of their old selves. I found myself being changed, responding to the gentle invitation of God, who in lovingkindness draws sinners to repentance. I saw that Christ took my shame, guilt, and unbelief upon himself. Reading the Scriptures, I saw how Jesus suffered, died, and was raised again to redeem sinners from false assumptions and lies. He endured the coldness of death that I might know the warmth of eternal life. I embraced this Jesus who died for me – even with all my enmeshment in homosexuality.

Shortly after leaving rehab, my lover moved to another state, unconvinced that God could love a homosexual and questioning how I could place my hope in such an unrealistic fantasy. I started attending a Bible-believing church where I was surprised both by the beauty of the worship and my acceptance by God's people. I found a Christian support group and began the painful process of looking at my sinful heart, with its lustful demands and multiple false assumptions. I grew in understanding my identity not as a "gay" but as a son of the living God. And God surprised me further when he called me back to school. With much fear, I returned to Philadelphia to attend Westminster Seminary. It was a great learning experience, and I continue to learn how to trust the faithfulness of God. Unlike the dark atmospheres inhabited by lonely men with fading roses and dying hopes, the light of God's love is found in the burning flames of his unfailing love and tender mercies.

Unexpected Present: Ministry

Today I am blessed to serve him who first loved me. I no longer define myself as "gay" or "homosexual" – or even as "ex-gay." I am a man defined by Christ and his righteousness and thus comfortable with my God-given maleness. I no longer chase fading yellow roses, but know the true and living hope that the Gospel brings. Indeed, I have scars, but I have learned not only to live with them but also to use them as a means of ministry, pointing others to the Scarred One.

I particularly have a heart to reach teens before they become more deeply enslaved in lies. I regularly extend this hope of the Gospel to those involved in homosexuality, their spouses, their parents, and their churches. The Almighty has made an inadequate and shamed man like me into a testimony of his grace, and it is now my privilege to be invited into the lives of other sinners so that I might tell them of the work of Christ. His truth and his love have set me free. Our God is fully able to do the impossible, and I continue to be surprised by Christ's grace.[22]

---

[22] After graduating from seminary, Rich worked with HARVEST USA for several years speaking on college campuses, debating pro-gay advocates, counseling men with same-sex attraction issues, leading support groups for men, and writing insightful critiques of our culture. Much to Rich's surprise, along the way he met Andrea at an "ex-gay" conference. When she described herself as the "whore at Christ's feet," he realized he had to get to know her. Neither was seeking a mate, nor expected to enter into a relationship with someone of the opposite sex, but God drew them together and they subsequently married.

Afterword

As you can tell from these stories, for most people, making the journey out of homosexuality toward Christ is a process of trusting God in new ways, one step at a time. It often involves just putting one foot in front of the other in obedience. For some of the writers, it was obedience unto death – they had to go through the suffering and pain of AIDS, even after trusting in the Lord. One might be bitter that Christ did not spare them suffering, especially since they had embraced him instead of their homosexuality. Yet they came to see that suffering is part of being conformed to the image of Christ. Christ suffered unto death for them, and so they could suffer unto death for him.

Of the individuals who are still among us on this side of the veil of death, the Christian walk continues. They would all confess that God isn't finished with them. They are not "free" of temptation, but then none of us are – even those who struggle with other sins like anger, gossip, pride. They aren't perfectly changed into what God wants them to be. Theirs is a life journey, similar to the one to which he calls us all. Those who would try to discredit anyone who is still tempted by sin as not really changed or as denying who he or she really is, frame the problem in the wrong way. They assume that if someone has changed he or she will no longer be tempted. Yet a thief is not a thief when he or she is tempted, but when he or she chooses to embrace the temptation and steal. So it is with sexual sins – be they homosexual or heterosexual. Leaving homosexuality is not about being free from temptation or becoming heterosexual, it is about living a life of holiness by faith. We are all called to holiness no matter what tempts us. We are all called to live by grace.

John Freeman, President
Harvest USA

About Harvest USA

Harvest USA began as a ministry of Tenth Presbyterian Church (PCA) in Philadelphia, PA, in 1983. It started as an outreach to the homosexual community located near the church. Staff members interacted with men and women in the area and started groups for individuals who wanted to get out of the homosexual lifestyle. Advertisements got the word out that such groups existed, and Harvest USA continued doing this type of direct ministry for many years.

Over time, it became apparent that a significant number of the individuals seeking help from Harvest USA were members of local churches who believed their own churches could not address their struggle. Harvest USA began to partner with churches, raising consciousness about the issues and creating a more grace-oriented environment.

Another transition occurred as staff members saw increasing numbers of individuals admitting struggles with "heterosexual" sins – viewing pornography, masturbation, extramarital sexual contacts, on-line affairs, using prostitutes, etc. Harvest USA began a support group for men struggling with these types of sins. It also created a group for wives to address the pain that they were enduring.

When it became apparent that the various types of sexual brokenness and sin that the staff was addressing came out of similar internal issues, the groups addressing homosexual and heterosexual struggles were folded together. This benefited all involved. To this day, individuals continue to seek assistance from Harvest USA through our regional offices and staff representatives.

Our culture continues to collapse in regard to sexual behaviors. This is fueled by the abundance of pornography on the Internet and strong political forces that oppose any form of restriction on sexual activity. The number of people with sexual sin struggles is growing rapidly both inside and outside the church. Statistical studies reveal there is virtually no difference between the sexual behaviors of individuals who profess a faith in Christ and those who do not. When it comes to sexuality, the church has, in many ways, become indistinguishable from the prevailing culture. It is critical that the church approach this issue from an historic, biblical perspective, address these issues, and respond with compassion and challenge.

Harvest USA has decades of experience addressing these issues from a biblical and compassionate position. It is clear to the staff and Board of Directors of Harvest USA that God is directing the ministry toward a new track. It is the vision of Harvest USA to see Christ heal a sexually broken world. For this to happen, the mission of Harvest USA is to partner with and equip the church in bringing the power of the Gospel of Jesus Christ to transform the lives of those affected by sexual sin.

Harvest USA is currently developing educational materials to assist the church in understanding and addressing these issues. The book you are reading is one in a series designed to address issues related to sexual brokenness and sin and how to minister to men and women struggling with these issues. Biblically based small group materials are also available for church-run support and accountability groups. Harvest USA staff is available to present seminars, teach Sunday school classes, preach, speak at retreats, breakfast meetings, and other groups, and do training. Our desire is to see a network of individuals and small groups, trained and equipped within the local church community; a network that will provide a place of genuine confession, healing, accountability, and growth in Christ.

For current information on all this, please go to the HARVEST USA website located at: www.harvestusa.org. Feel free to contact us directly at info@harvestusa.org.

Need Help?

If the contents of this book have stirred up spiritual and emotional issues within you, it is important to share this with someone you trust. We encourage you to speak with someone you trust at your church. It is important, however, that you not share deep inner hurts and struggles with just anyone – some people can do more harm than good because of where they are in their own spiritual growth process. Prayerfully and deliberately consider someone who consistently displays love and grace to others, as well as a commitment to biblical authority.

If you want to speak to someone at HARVEST USA, you are welcome to call us. Check our website – www.harvestusa.org – for the phone number of the office closest to you.

Need More Copies?

If you found this book helpful and need more copies, please go to www.harvestusa.org to order. You will find other resources and links on the website.

Support Us

Harvest USA is a non-profit ministry that relies almost completely on the donations of individuals and churches, along with gifts from supportive businesses and foundations. We do not charge people seeking our help. The fees charged for our seminars and training events are designed to cover our costs.

Harvest USA is a mission work, proclaiming hope in Christ and partnering with churches and individuals to address issues of sexual sin. This kind of ministry and support philosophy has its challenges. We do not know what our income will be on any given day. We want to invite you to consider if God might be moving you to be one of our partners-in-ministry through your financial support. Please also consider advocating for Harvest USA with your church's mission committee or with anyone else you know who could help. We encourage you to pray about how God might use you. For more information, contact our Development Director through our website at: www.harvestusa.org. He is located at our Philadelphia office. If you have found this book helpful, would like to give us feedback, or want to support the ministry, you can contact us on the web or at our Philadelphia address.

Harvest USA
3901-B Main Street, Suite 304
Philadelphia, PA 19127

Phone: 215-482-0111

E-mail: info@harvestusa.org

Website: www.harvestusa.org